giraffeMONEY

Chris Jarvis

Michelle
Be the Giraffe!

A GIRAFFE UNIVERSITY PRESS BOOK

giraffeMONEY

See Better Paths to Elevated Wealth

Chris Jarvis, MBA, CFP

© 2020 All Rights Reserved

ISBN: 9798648916210

Cover design by Ramón E. Peralta, Jr., Peralta Design

Interior design and composition by MikeLoomis.CO

No part of this book may be reproduced, stored in a retrieval system, or transmitted by any means without the written permission of the author and publisher.

In memory of my dad,

Ray Jarvis
May 10, 1946 – April 24, 2020

Thank you for encouraging me to take risks,
climb the highest mountains, and never look back.

Contents

Foreword by Jack Canfield

I never wanted to be a giraffe—until I met Chris Jarvis.

I've known Chris for years, having interviewed him for *Hollywood Live* and *Talking about Success*. It was during our last interview that Chris explained to me that I was already "Being the giraffe." He told me that his billionaire and multi-millionaire clients all attribute their success to sticking their necks out when other people chose to remain in the safety of the herd. This is exactly what I did when I refused to take no for an answer (even after 144 unsuccessful pitches) for my big idea – Chicken Soup for the Soul!

I'm always impressed with Chris's ability to simplify and effectively communicate very complicated ideas. He has a no-BS approach to business and life, and an impressive drive to make a positive difference in the lives of others.

As the co-author of the bestselling *Chicken Soup for the Soul®* series, I have had the opportunity to author or co-author more than 170 books (47 of which are *New York Times* bestsellers). That success has afforded me the opportunity to work with hundreds of thousands of people all over the world, and among all those people, Chris stands out—like a giraffe on the plains. Unlike many of the people in the financial world, he does not measure his success just by dollars earned. Chris is first and foremost a teacher who wants to help people enjoy their success by eliminating the unnecessary stress and aggravation that often accompany financial success. His motives are pure, and his advice is unbiased.

After selling his company for millions of dollars in 2016, Chris surprised me again by signing up for my Train the Trainer program. By the time our year-long program was over, Chris wasn't just a trainer. He had stood out (or above) and we named him the Vice President of Strategic Partnerships for the Canfield Training Group. Chris's giraffe-like vision allowed him to see a unique path to success that combines financial, entrepreneurial and transformational elements. This is why this book is so exciting for me and for you.

Over the past 45 years, I have been helping people do what giraffes have been doing for over a million years – evolving to become *more* vulnerable. While every other herbivore has evolved to hide or protect its most vulnerable area, the giraffe has developed the longest neck in the animal kingdom. As a result of this vulnerability, giraffes can see things others can't and can reach things others won't. I teach the importance of opening up and becoming vulnerable so you can create connections and grow as a person. Chris took that lesson to heart and creatively applied it to personal finance in a way that is easy to understand and incredibly impactful when applied.

Chris Jarvis with Jack Canfield, December 2019

In giraffeMONEY, Chris shares seven paths to move away from the herd-mentality. You'll learn how the super-affluent people in our country are very different from average Americans—just as giraffes are very different from zebras. Apart from the obvious (higher incomes and longer necks), giraffes see differently, feed differently, move differently, and interact differently than all other herd animals do. To be super successful you want to be an outlier financially – away from the rest of the herd. To do so, you will have to resist the urge to fit in.

Widely accepted financial advice may be appropriate for average or moderately successful Americans, but that same advice can be financially detrimental for people who are trying to reach elevated levels of wealth. The broad acceptance of conventional wisdom is the most devastating factor when it comes to financial planning for affluent families.

Unlike the millions of migrating herd animals who wander endlessly following the seasonal rains to find new grasses, giraffes eat tender, green leaves from trees. Since trees have roots that can access underground moisture, they grow in places where grass simply will not. As a result, the giraffe can survive and even thrive in very barren places (like a desert) where herd animals could never survive.

In today's challenging times, you may want to take a different path and achieve better results. gira*ffe*MONEY offers you many different paths that will be much more than an oasis for you. You will learn how to change your mindset, implement advanced financial strategies, and avoid catastrophic mistakes.

You will also learn what types of advisors can help you and how they work. You will learn how to identify if you have outgrown particular advisors or firms. Most importantly, you will learn how to work more efficiently with lawyers, accountants, and financial advisors so you avoid conflicts of interest, reduce costs, and maximize the value you receive.

I have come to deeply trust Chris and his advice. That's why I proudly wrote the Foreword for Chris's last bestseller—*6 Secrets to Leveraging Success: A Guide for Entrepreneurs, Family Offices and Their Trusted Advisors.* I have trusted Chris Jarvis to represent my company, my brand and me. If you want to see a better path to earning more income or amassing greater wealth than 99% of the population, you are going to have to stick your neck out and do something different. I suggest that you too trust Chris Jarvis to teach you how to do that by reading gira*ffe*MONEY.

I wish you well on your new paths to new heights of success.

Jack Canfield
Coauthor of the bestselling *Chicken Soup for the Soul®* series and
The Success Principles™: How to Get from Where You Are to Where You Want to Be

Why Successful People Became Giraffes First

"Every success story is a tale of constant adaptation, revision and change."

—Richard Branson

Since the publication of my first book over twenty years ago, much has changed. The psychological and financial chasm between the rich and the middle class has dramatically expanded. Americans used to idolize the super affluent and aspire to follow in their footsteps. Some would call that sentiment capitalism at its finest. Consider that *Lifestyles of the Rich and Famous* was once a top-rated television program that featured extravagant wealth and the toys that came with such success. Its host Robin Leach would sign off each episode wishing you "champagne wishes and caviar dreams."

Fast forward to today. The wealthiest one percent have been the subject of many political candidates' campaigns and national budget discussions, debating perspectives on their incomes and tax liabilities. In a strange turn of events, the most successful Americans are often perceived as villains by some popular media. As a result, the wealthy are less open about their success and the methods they have used to achieve affluence. Understandably, the super successful don't want the proverbial bullseye on their backs.

Not only are the rich keeping their mouths shut, but corporations and professional service firms now have what I call "institutional laryngitis." Investment firms, insurance companies, law firms, and accounting firms are all struggling with declining margins creating extreme pressure to streamline operations. To boost confidence, they brag to shareholders or investors about their sizable investments and commitment to leverage technology. What does that mean to you? When you read or hear "leverage technology," you should think "less human interaction, no personal customization."

Henry Ford once said about the Model-T, "You can have any color you like, as long as it's black." In the industrial revolution, machines were built to do one task very well. The goal was to increase production at a reduced cost. Later, we became obsessed with customization, until it was too expensive. Technology advances are causing service industries to evolve, and it looks like history is repeating itself.

Attorneys use WealthDocs or HotDocs to kick out legal documents. Accounting firms now use tax return software. Insurance companies have to get all of their products filed and approved by state insurance departments (and their competitors can see the details of the filings), so nobody is "different" very long. Investment firms are offering the same securities or are packaging combinations of investments and significantly increasing the fees. No matter how you slice it, most service industries are giving you the same service as their competitors but are charging you for customization you aren't receiving.

Who can you turn to for help? Local newspapers and news stations once had investigative reporters looking out for consumers. Now, the media is far less credible—especially when it comes to scrutinizing the companies whose ads pay their salary. Regardless of your political ideology, it is clear that media have shifted from pure unbiased reporting of facts toward spinning news that appeals to their demographic. The point is that people can't trust what they read about the economy, the stock market, or the government's role and impact on either.

You need information. Good information. Forget searching the internet for advice. A Google search yielding 20,000,000 results is *useless*. You need *useful, manageable,* applicable knowledge. You need to find someone to guide you on this journey. If you are not Elon Musk, or can't find a mentor like Warren Buffett to teach you how to build a fortune, where will you turn for this invaluable advice?

Enter the Giraffe

Some of my fondest memories are of nature shows. As a child, my father and I would watch Mutual of Omaha's Wild Kingdom. In high school, I was a fixture at my best friend Rob Whelan's house on Nelson Street in the working-class Elmhurst section of Providence, Rhode Island. I was there so often that his parents, Bob and Dotty, named me "Skippy" (see the popular Michael J. Fox tv show, *Family Ties* as a reference), and they still call me that over 30 years later. When at their house, I would often watch National Geographic specials with his dad Bob.

Fast forward to 2002. I had the opportunity to take the trip of a lifetime. I went on safari to South Africa, Botswana, Zimbabwe, and Zambia with my father Ray and my dear friend Lee Kaplan. Like most people, I was so excited to view lions in the wild. But, one day in Botswana at Chobe National Park, we stumbled on a tower of giraffes. The sheer size and majesty were beyond description, but the giraffes' characteristics and behavior were so remarkable and memorable, that they became the foundation for **gira*ffe*MONEY**, ***Be the Giraffe***, GiraffeUniversity.com, and my lucrative consulting practice.

Chobe, Botswana. 2002. Me, Mist, Ray Jarvis, Eric, Lee Kaplan.

One of the first things you learn watching nature shows is that some animals eat other animals. My dad explained to me that—over time—this predator and prey game makes the animals stronger. I learned that predators have adapted and become faster, stronger, or more efficient hunters. They developed camouflage, stalking techniques, and excellent night vision. I also learned that "prey" animals have evolved to "protect" themselves better—the ones who didn't are now extinct.

How have most animals evolved to protect themselves from more dominant and stronger predators? Some animals have developed hard shells or a very thick hide, while others have sharp quills or exude a poisonous secretion. Each of these characteristics is designed by nature to prevent the fatal bite to the neck. The giraffe is a whole different animal—literally. Through evolution, the giraffe has *expanded* its most vulnerable area: its neck. That sounds crazy, but it worked. How?

The giraffe, despite its increased vulnerability, has developed something valuable that no other land animal has. With a head that reaches up to 20 feet off the ground, the giraffe has an elevated perspective that allows it to see over bushes, small trees, and all the other animals who are living with their heads in the weeds. It can see opportunity or danger much further off in the distance than other animals. The benefits are not only vision. Height also gives the tallest mammal a private dining room. The giraffe eats leaves high up in the trees which is food the millions of other grazing animals on the plains will never reach.

How might being a giraffe help you with your money?

Would you like to see paths to success that others can't? Would it be helpful if you could see approaching threats long before other investors or competitors do? Would you like to reach levels your competitors and colleagues never will?

When you decide to "Be a Giraffe," you will stick your neck out and become more vulnerable, but your elevated vision will help you reap the rewards—while those who play it safe wander in nervous herds.

My Perspective

My books and seminars have reached tens of thousands of Americans, and my articles have been read by hundreds of thousands more. Not surprisingly, thousands of strangers, ranging from highly educated physicians and attorneys to high school dropouts worth $500 million, have contacted my offices asking for financial advice in one capacity or another. They've worked with the herd but wanted a different perspective.

This unique opportunity to meet people from all areas of the country introduced me to hundreds of attorneys, accountants, and financial advisors who represented those strangers before they contacted us. The primary purpose of our communication was to learn more about the clients' specific circumstances. The secondary, and completely unintentional (at the time) goal was to collect thousands of valuable case studies to help write this book.

There are many ways that people can earn very attractive incomes. You could sell ball bearings, popcorn boxes, or specialty valves and circuits for mining equipment for instance. We all face our share of financial adversity as well. Global crisis, disabling injuries, divorce, and lawsuits are the most common causes, but competitive and regulatory forces can also be crippling, if not catastrophic. What is amazing is how some people are able to continue the accumulation of wealth while experiencing catastrophes that have wiped out less-savvy families. What they know allows them to go far beyond success and achieve super-affluence. Working with a diverse collection of these clients and their talented advisors helped me uncover tricks of the trade to build and preserve wealth in any economic climate. These are the "Giraffe Money Secrets" that you need to master to reach the highest levels of affluence.

In this information age, where everything is a few keystrokes search away, you may be skeptical that there are any secrets remaining. With millions of financial advisors, insurance agents, attorneys, and accountants competing for your business, there shouldn't be any stone left unturned. Generally speaking, you are right. Despite the readily available nature of the tools, we see so few families and businesses applying the right combination of tools and strategies to maximize income and wealth.

According to the IRS and Bloomberg, as reported in *Forbes* on 10/22/2019:

- Half of Americans earned > $41,740 in 2017.
- Fewer than 5% of households earned > $208,000 in 2017.
- Fewer than 1% of households earned > $515,000 in 2017.
- Only 1 in 1,000 households earned > $2,374,937 in 2017.
- There were 675,000 new millionaires in the US in 2017.
- There are now over 18.6 million Americans who are millionaires.

There are two take-away messages. First, there are proven paths to building and preserving wealth over multiple generations. Second, a small percentage of people actually take the steps necessary to do it. Which group will you be in:

- Half the population, struggling to earn more than $42,000 per year?
- 19 of 20 people who are hoping to earn more than $208,000 per year?
- 1 in 1,000 who earn more than $2.3 million per year?
- One of the 675,000 new millionaires in the United States next year?

Regardless of where you set your sights, **giraffeMONEY** will teach you the two most important concepts for building wealth, explain dozens of philosophies, techniques and tools for use in your planning to identify the risks to long-term success, and offer ways to protect yourself from them. These lessons are essential for those who want to be wealthy, those who are already wealthy—and the professional advisors who want to differentiate themselves from the millions of other advisors who are competing to serve the wealthiest clients.

Conveniently, **giraffeMONEY** offers all of this valuable information along seven Paths. Within each path, there are a number of valuable lessons. Here is a preview of what you will learn from **giraffeMONEY.**

1. How super successful people look at things differently
2. The single most important strategy for getting more out of your career
3. What five things kill most businesses – and how can you avoid them all
4. How to eliminate unnecessary taxes in every area of your life
5. How to get more out of your time, money and assets
6. How to avoid firms and professionals who may take advantage of you
7. Why most people fall short of their goals and how to change that today!

You are on your own path, but you are truly never alone. For regular support, additional resources, and a network of like-minded people who want to see you succeed, visit us at www.GiraffeUniversity.com and subscribe to my newsletter.

When you elevate your perspective, you can see a better path – for you!

Be the Giraffe!

Chris Jarvis
www.ChrisJarvis.me
Founder, Giraffe University
www. GiraffeUniversity.com

1st PATH
What Do Giraffes Know about Money?

"Evolution is so creative. That is how we got giraffes."
—Kurt Vonnegut

Rather than throw you right into the financial tools and strategies of the rich and famous, I want you first to understand some important "giraffe-isms." Giraffes may not have bank accounts, stock portfolios, or a family office. However, the evolution of thc giraffe and its current lifestyle most closely mirrors the most successful people I have worked with in my career.

When I sold my company in 2016 for millions of dollars, two of my mentors challenged me. Jay Abraham and Jack Canfield independently told me, "Writing about how you were successful *might* be interesting but discovering lessons that anyone could use *will* be impactful." Talking to clients and reflecting on my path, I found universal lessons that applied to all super successful people. As I wrote them all down on the whiteboards that line "my lab" in my home, it jumped out at me. These people are all giraffes!

You will see the shocking similarities between the wealthiest people in our country and the tallest animals on the planet. More interestingly, you will see how the majority of Americans act like herd animals – such as zebra and wildebeest.

Once you know what it means to be a giraffe, you will better appreciate how giraffe characteristics will help you reach your most ambitious financial goals. As you stick your neck out, you will develop an elevated perspective on money, business, and life.

This perspective will help you answer these questions:

1) What does it take to become wealthy in America?
2) Why don't more people become more successful?
3) What conventional wisdom is detrimental to affluence?

4) What unusual things are the richest people doing and why I haven't heard of them? (Perhaps you are skeptical about the existence of such strategies.)

You will see the answers to these important questions and notice other details that may prove helpful on your journey. This foundation will change how you think about, and look at, wealth and success. This elevated perspective will help you more easily absorb and better utilize the information in the book (and the supporting materials at GiraffeUniversity.com) to help you build your fortune, increase your impact, and leave a greater legacy.

Chapter 1
How Are Wealthy People like Giraffes?

"Wealth is the product of man's capacity to think."

—Ayn Rand

The focus of this book is to teach you how to *be a giraffe* so you can reach your ambitious financial goals. Perhaps you want to reach financial independence for yourself or your family. Maybe you are looking to increase your net worth by millions—or tens of millions of dollars. Either way, you will benefit from seeing the similarities between the wealthiest people and the tallest animal.

We must understand why we are sticking our necks outs in the first place. We are trying to elevate our perspectives so we can see a better path. We want to see and follow a better path to wealth and happiness. When people have stuck their necks out, have taken chances by doing things differently, and have reached the highest levels of success, we refer to them as "giraffes."

You need to compare the giraffe to its fellow mammals before you can appreciate their special qualities. To simplify the population, we'll herd everyone into two categories: giraffes and zebra. The quickest way to determine a giraffe versus a zebra is to check the height. In the wild, there is no confusion between the two, as a zebra is 4 to 6 feet tall, and a giraffe is 14 to 20 feet tall. In this financial book, the height we are talking about is the size of your money stacked up in front of you. If you earn a lot of money, or have amassed a significant net worth, consider yourself a giraffe.

Second, we can see if you are a zebra or a giraffe based on an "eye exam." This is not like the test you took in grade school or, the more recent one I took as I approach 50 and finally need glasses. This eye exam tests your vision for yourself, your business, and your life. In the wild, zebra eat grass and spend most of their days with their eyes a few feet—or a few inches—

off the ground. Giraffes spend as much of their days eating, but munch leaves from the tops of trees.

Giraffes have a unique perspective and see both opportunities and threats long before other herbivores. If you are a step ahead of your colleagues, or do things differently because you see things differently, you may be deemed a giraffe based on *how* you achieved your success.

Whether you are already a giraffe, hope to become more giraffe-like, or plan to work with giraffes as a financial, legal, or tax advisor, you will find valuable philosophical and practical insights along the seven paths in this book. You may find some the lessons apply to you right now—but as you grow and your circumstances change, revisiting some of the paths may be very helpful.

Giraffe Earners

Giraffe earners are those who stand out among those around them. The same way the giraffe is more than ten feet taller than the zebra on the plain, giraffe earners stand far above. Based on IRS and Bloomberg data from 2017, roughly one percent of Americans earned more than $500,000 – much more than the zebra we will examine later.

As the previous owner of two financial and insurance firms, and the author of over a dozen books on financial planning, I have met with hundreds of giraffe earners in my career. The significant income disparity causes the giraffe earners to have different financial concerns than zebra. Generally, these challenges include growing their businesses, avoiding financial catastrophes, reducing taxes, managing investments, and coordinating multiple advisers. These topics will be discussed in greater detail within each of the seven paths in **giraffeMONEY**.

Giraffes in Botswana, 2002.

Giraffe Builders

Giraffes have numerous unique qualities, but they do not have opposable thumbs. I am unaware of any anecdotal evidence of giraffes "going primate" and learning to use tools. With that said, the giraffe metaphor works when we consider the "giraffe" to be the adjective and not the noun. Any person or family that has amassed more than $10,000,000 in net worth is called a giraffe builder because of their unusually tall net worth. I've had the pleasure of working with three billionaire families and hundreds of millionaires. From personal experience, I have helped giraffe builders address many of the same concerns of giraffe earners, but they do have some unique challenges. Very wealthy families are concerned with estate taxes and protecting their children's and grandchildren's future inheritances from divorce and other litigation. They are also concerned with teaching their children how to appreciate what they have, so they don't squander their fortunate upbringing and future assets.

Builders May or May Not Be Earners (Anymore)

We acknowledge that many people will fall into both categories. The giraffe earners may invest wisely and become giraffe builders, or giraffe builders may earn enough from their investments to be categorized as giraffe earners—but this is not always the case. Therefore, I don't use only net worth or income as an indicator of success. For example, a second-year neurosurgeon may earn $600,000 per year (source: www.mdsalaries.blogspot.com) but may not pay off all of her educational debt and begin to save money for a number of years. We did not think it accurate to categorize her as a zebra, despite relatively low net worth. She is a giraffe earner because of her unusually high income.

Similarly, a man who sold his business for $50 million, quit working, and lives off his tax-free municipal bond portfolio doesn't appear to resemble a zebra. He doesn't have a job and has $0 of taxable income, but his high net worth certainly causes him to stand apart from most people. Although both of these giraffes stand out among most Americans, you can also appreciate that the neurosurgeon may have very different concerns from the young retiree, and different paths in **giraffeMONEY** may prove more beneficial to one than the other.

Giraffe Elders

Giraffe earners and giraffe builders are titles based on the amount of income or net worth of a person or family. This category, *giraffe elder,* is reserved for persons, families, or businesses that have learned valuable lessons and led by example. Every builder or earner is not someone you want your children or grandchildren to mimic (see Hilton, Paris, or Kardashian, Kim). Inheriting money or profiting from shameless self-promotion may not be the lessons you want to share with your heirs.

By speaking to thousands of earners and builders, and working with hundreds of professionals across the country, I have witnessed countless creative ways to grow, build, and preserve wealth. I have also seen how carelessness or procrastination can cost families millions—or tens of millions—of dollars in unnecessary taxes, legal expenses, and lost income.

Important Note: Many of the philosophies in this book are universal and are applicable in any city, state, province, or country. These lessons are passed down within wealthy families and empires and have been for thousands of years. Many of the practical tips in the areas of asset protection, tax, and estate planning are based on the laws of the United States and will apply to anyone living in this country.

Charting a Better Path

Giraffes are the tallest animals in the wild. Humans who become the largest earners and who accumulate the most significant wealth are the "giraffes" who stand out in our society. Similar to how the animal has evolved over millions of years, business owners and families who make slight adjustments to how they think about and approach wealth will eventually see themselves standing much higher on the socioeconomic ladder than those who are unwilling to stick their necks out to see a better path.

Now that you understand the main idea behind, and the benefits of, being a giraffe, you are almost ready to begin your practical training and learn the secrets to reaching your financial goals. Before you take steps toward your own financial evolution, you need to appreciate why you don't want to remain where you are. It is imperative you fully understand why I call average Americans "zebra," how most firms and media outlets cater to the more numerous zebra, and how listening to zebra will only confuse you as you try to elevate your perspective.

Chapter 2
Zebras in America. Who Knew?

"Be careful when following the masses. Sometimes the 'm' is silent."
—Unknown

Before you can understand what, why, and how giraffes are so different, you need to understand the qualities and actions of the vast herds of zebra standing all around the giraffes on the plains. Zebra have small family units of 5 to 20 animals that congregate with other families in herds of thousands of other animals. Giraffes, on the other hand, are solitary animals that socialize in "towers" temporarily.

Zebra migrate over thousands of miles, following the rains that lead to enough grass for these large herds to feed. Giraffes are non-migratory and non-territorial. They only need enough food for themselves. They eat the leaves of trees, and trees have roots that access water well below the soil. Therefore, giraffes can find food in places herd animals simply cannot.

Zebra represent large groups of Americans who make up 90 percent of the population. Like zebra who are constantly migrating to find its next meal, most Americans have similar challenges (living paycheck to paycheck). If a zebra tries to leave the safety of the herd, it doesn't have the resources to protect itself from the predators. Similarly, most Americans can't afford to quit their jobs, seek additional training, and pursue another career. In many ways, most Americans are stuck in their jobs and careers the same way the zebra have no choice but to stay in the herd.

Perhaps, you now realize that giraffes are more independent, have more options, and have greater flexibility. These are keys to achieving high levels of financial success.

Important Note: Throughout this book, we use the terms *zebra* and *average Americans.* To some, this term may seem to be demeaning or condescending or to infer a value judgment. It is not intended that way. It is a simple metaphor to point out that there are a lot more zebra than giraffes and that those few giraffes stand out (financially) among the larger group of zebra.

How Much Does a Zebra Make?

The first and perhaps most important defining characteristic of the average American (zebra) is income level. The median income for a family in the United States was $63,030 in 2019. This is down slightly (0.45%) from $63,314 in 2018. Median means that half of US households earned more than $63,030 and half earned more than $63,030 in 2019. Averages are misleading, so I prefer not to use them. Let me explain why then we can move on and dissect the population further.

> **The Mathematician Can't (or Won't) Divide by Three (3)**
> If you and I were on stage with Bill Gates, it would likely be correct to say, "the average net worth of the three people on stage is over $34 billion." It may be accurate, but also misleading. That statement might lead someone to believe that you and I are not only billionaires, but that we are two of the richest people in the world. The truth is that, unless you are a multi-billionaire yourself, more than 99.9% of the total net worth on stage would belong to Bill Gates. When there are significant outliers in any group, the median will give you a much more accurate estimate of the "typical" or average person in the group.

Let's break the US Populations income in 2019 a bit further so we can get a better idea of how, and why, the financial and consulting industries have failed us*†:

- 25% earned less than $31,201
- 25% between $31,201 and $63,030
- 25% earned between $63,030 and $113,010
- 15% earned between$113,010 and $184,200
- 10% earned $184,200 or more in 2019 (up 0.6% from 2018)
- 5% earned $248,304 or more in 2019 (up 2.6% from 2018)
- 1% earned $475,116 or more in 2019 (up 6.8% from 2018)
- Average income among all U.S. households: $89,931

*Source: https://dqydj.com/household-income-percentile-calculator/
†Households may include two or more earners.

Another way to look at this is to look at groups.

39,162,447 households (30,4%) earned > $100,000 in 2019.

6,365,893 households (4.9%) earned > $250,000 in 2019.

The significance of this income analysis is relatively simple. Average Americans are generally earning just enough to pay the bills. In many areas of the country, where expenses are comparatively high, most Americans are not earning enough income to cover their bills. Consider this very troubling data from *before* the economic impact of the coronavirus quarantine:

> Total household debt in the United States, including mortgages, auto loans, credit card and student debt, climbed to $14.15 trillion in the fourth quarter of 2019, eclipsing the previous peak at the height of the great recession in Q3 2008 by $1.5 trillion in nominal terms.
>
> —Federal Reserve Bank of New York's Report on Household Debt and Credit
>
> https://www.newyorkfed.org/microeconomics/hhdc.html

Long-term uses of income, such as funding retirement accounts, paying insurance premiums, and funding college savings accounts are luxuries many average Americans simply cannot afford.

Giraffes Adapt to Their Habitat

Nationwide income disparity only tells part of the story. There is significant disparity in income from state to state. This is an important variable because it requires surplus income to be able to make money *on* your money. You create more investment leverage if you can earn more or less.

Consider the minimum income threshold to be included in the top one percent of earners in each state. On the left side of the chart, you will see the ten states with the highest minimal income thresholds to be in the top one percent of all earners in that state. On the right side, you can see the states with the lowest qualifying income thresholds to reach the top one percent of earners in those states.

What Do the Top 1% Earn in Each State?

State	At Least	State	At Least
Connecticut	$678k	Arkansas	$228k
District of Columbia	$555k	New Mexico	$241k
New Jersey	$539k	West Virginia	$243k
Massachusetts	$532k	Mississippi	$263k
New York	$506k	Kentucky	$263k
North Dakota	$502k	Alabama	$272k
California	$438k	Maine	$274k
Illinois	$424k	South Carolina	$275k
Texas	$423k	Hawaii	$279k
Maryland	$419k	Idaho	$280k

Source: Adapted from Estelle Sommeiller and Mark Price, *The Increasingly Unequal States of America: Income Inequality by State, 1917 to 2012*, an Economic Analysis and Research Network (EARN) report published January 26, 2015.

Go.epi.org/unequalstates

To ensure you are reading the table properly, I offer this brief explanation. In Connecticut, one in every 100 of the residents will earn at least $678,000 per year. By sharp contrast, only one percent of Arkansas residents earn more than $228,000.

At first glance, most of the data in the last table makes perfect sense. You might expect there to be a lot of people living in and around New York who have very high salaries – making the top one percent threshold quite high. You were probably unsurprised by the low thresholds in many Southern states – where the cost of living is much lower, and poverty is widespread.

Federal Income Tax Rates

The second defining characteristic of the average American is federal income tax rates. As you will see later in the book, affluent Americans consider taxes in nearly everything they do because their tax rates can be very high, and tax expense can be the primary drag on their quest for super affluence. Contrast that to the situation of average Americans. If you combine the household demographics stated above with the 2020 Federal tax rate schedule below, for married couples filing jointly, you can draw some interesting conclusions.

Married filing jointly and surviving spouses for 2020	
If Taxable Income Is	**The Tax Is**
Not more than $19,750	10% of the taxable income
More than $19,751, but not more than $80,250	$1,975 plus 12% of the amount in excess of $19,750
More than $80,251, but not more than $171,050	$9,235 plus 22% of the amount in excess of $80,250
More than $171,051, but not more than $326,600	$29,211 plus 24% of the amount in excess of $171,050
More than $326,601, but not more than $414,700	$66,543 plus 32% of the amount in excess of $326,600
More than $414,701, but not over $622,050	$94,735 plus 35% of the amount in excess of $414,700
More than $622,051	$167,307.50 plus 37% of the amount in excess of $622.050

You can estimate that approximately 60 percent of the population will pay less than 12 percent of their adjusted gross income in federal income taxes. The tax is up to 12 percent of their *taxable* income (after the standard and other allowable deductions). Another 37 percent of the population will pay less than 20 percent of their taxable income to the federal government via income taxes. The remaining three percent of the population will earn enough to pay more than 20 percent of their adjusted gross income in taxes. Since all taxable income in excess of $622,050 is subject to federal income tax rates of 37 percent, a couple earning $1,000,000 per year will pay 31 percent in federal income taxes. A couple earning $2,000,000 per year will pay 34% in federal income taxes.

In other words, average Americans pay relatively few dollars in income taxes as a percentage of their income. For this reason, income tax planning is not as significant a concern for the average American as it is for a super-affluent family that is paying income taxes of 31 to 34 percent. It's no surprise that turning over one of every three dollars earned motivated the *giraffe earners* to make tax planning a priority and to get very creative.

Referee and Other Zebra Jobs

The third defining characteristic of average Americans is their source of income. The average American is almost always an employee who works for someone else. Note: there are many self-employed independent contractors in the population. These could be skilled laborers, salespersons, or other technical or part-time employees who are not legally considered employees. They may have even fewer benefits than employed workers. They are considered part of the zebra population as I make this point.

Employed workers are paid as *W-2 employees* and may or may not have modest benefits packages. Taxes are typically withheld from the average American's paycheck each payday, before after-tax proceeds are distributed. Many refer to this as your *take-home* pay.

While this system eliminates the headaches of calculating and preparing complex quarterly estimated tax payments and needing to save for these large payments, there is little opportunity for significant tax planning. The average American rarely owns a business. This means that the average American does not have to manage a growing or complicated business that may have multiple locations, many employees, and regulatory reporting requirements. This also means that the average American's income is determined by someone else. The employing company determines when and if there are raises or promotions for employees. Employees can work hard, but the financial rewards for such efforts are at the discretion of someone else. Because the cost-of-living increases every year, modest raises may provide relatively modest increased spending and saving potential over a lifetime.

Millions of Americans have made the decision to buy or build a small business. There are countless motivations that drive someone to leave the world of the employed to start or run a business. There are pros and cons to working for someone else instead of running your own business, as you can see in the following table:

Pros and Cons of Working for Someone Else	
Pros of Being an Employee	**Cons of Being an Employee**
Simplified tax reporting	Little opportunity for tax planning
Fixed or predictable income	Little opportunity for significant increases in income
Benefits managed by employer	No control over benefits offered
Job stability	Job stability controlled by employer
Employer leverages your work	No direct benefit from leverage
Little lawsuit risk as compared to the employer	Probably don't earn enough to be a target
No business succession risk	No business to leave for heirs

No doubt, running a business is hard work and is certainly not for everyone. The risks associated with owning a business are validated by the fact that most small businesses fail. However, there are some tradeoffs that are worth the risk to entrepreneurs. Employees have little say in planning for the business. Though employees have less risk, they also have less opportunity for financial upside. There is no universal better or worse. It is just the nature of the situation. This is one of the ways that average Americans who are employees differ from business owners who have the greater opportunity to achieve affluence.

Can a Zebra Retire?

The fourth area of difference between the average and affluent Americans is in the area of retirement planning. For nearly a century, a major goal of employment for average Americans has been to save enough money to retire. Most Americans look forward to doing something other than working, and many anticipate financial freedom in retirement.

For retirement planning, most average Americans invest in some type of retirement plan offered by their employer, typically a 401(k) plan. Most average Americans also have checking and savings accounts, and possibly an individual retirement account (IRA) or small investment account. However, they do not have substantial or sufficient savings in such accounts. This is the result of a combination of factors such as:

- People are living longer and requiring income for more years in retirement, and therefore more savings.
- Employers are focused on quarterly earnings and are forced to cut back on employee benefits, including retirement funding.

- Reduced benefits for health care coverage from employers causes increased spending by the employees' families. Average Americans are spending more on consumer purchases than on retirement plans simply because their incomes don't afford them the opportunity to do both. When companies give less to employees and the employees have to spend more to pay the bills, the employees do not have the discretionary funds to save enough for their desired level of retirement and cannot put enough money into these savings plans.
- Many Americans are still be relying on Social Security to provide a large portion of their retirement income. You need only read a week's worth of articles in the publications listed later in this chapter to get a clear understanding that relying on Social Security is not a sufficient planning decision for most Americans. Yet, most average Americans have few or no retirement alternatives.

Zebra Protect Their Asses, not Their Assets

Besides estate tax planning, asset protection is the area of financial planning where the needs and concerns of average Americans and affluent Americans differ most. Asset protection—the practice of shielding wealth from potential lawsuits, creditors, or other claims—is plainly not of significant concern to average Americans for two reasons:

1. Most do not have substantial assets to protect.
2. Most do not face significant liability through their work or as a result of their investments.

You've probably heard, "the bigger you are, the harder you fall." For giraffes who have a lot to lose, they are understandably more concerned with becoming the target of big game hunting lawyers. Protecting what you have is a critical factor in financial planning for very successful Americans. We are only touching on this briefly here. You will see many ways to protect yourself, your business, and your family wealth from a variety of catastrophic risks along the 3rd Path of **gira*ffe*MONEY**.

Zebra Estate Plan

Under today's laws, an individual's heirs will only be subject to Federal estate taxes if that individual has an estate worth more than $11,580,000. If a couple is married, and they utilize a very easy, effective, and underutilized planning technique, they can legally pass up to $23,160,000 to heirs with no gift or estate taxes. Further, by utilizing one particular estate planning document (take a stroll down the 6th Path of **giraffeMONEY**), a family can significantly reduce estate taxes on inheritances above these values.

As recently as 2011, however, the exemption amount (for estate tax purposes) was as low as $1 million per person ($2 million per couple). Why do we mention this? The estimated costs of the coronavirus (CoVid-19) at the time of this writing were in excess of $1 trillion. Those dollars will have to be recouped through taxes. Comments on the future of estate taxes and why we should expect much higher tax rates and lower exemption amounts in the future will be offered later in this book.

With 90 percent of households earning less than $185,000 per year, it is highly unlikely that most Americans are concerned about estate taxes under the current law. After most American families pay their living expenses, raise children, pay educational costs for children, secure a retirement, handle the unforeseen financial burdens we all encounter during our lifetimes, how much will they have to invest? It is possible that a zebra could get lucky, or be very smart, and accumulate more than $23 million to leave to children as an inheritance, but the odds are pretty slim. As a result, estate tax planning (focused on reducing inheritance and wealth transfer tax liabilities) is not a major concern of the average American family.

There are three cautionary tales here. First, there could be a shift in power in Washington resulting in a major change to the exemption amount. This could require many more Americans to be subject to estate taxes in the future. Second, states have begun to implement their own inheritance taxes which come into effect at much lower levels than federal estate taxes. Third, many of the estate planning tools that super-affluent families utilize to reduce estate taxes have other benefits that all of us would like to enjoy such as privacy of family affairs when someone dies, elimination of unnecessary fees and aggravation at death, and protection of an inheritance from divorce or lawsuits. Even if you never plan to be worth $11 million, the 4th Path **giraffeMONEY** is an important one for you to stroll down to learn some valuable tips.

Charting a Better Path

Average Americans do not have as many opportunities to enhance their financial situations as do affluent Americans. Average Americans must spend most of what they earn on living expenses and what little is left goes to income taxes (albeit at a relatively low rate). As an employee or an owner running a small business, the zebra has neither the opportunity to use many tax-saving vehicles nor the flexibility to create their own benefits programs.

The zebra family has precious few retirement assets and minimal risk of losing assets to judgment creditors. Upon death, nearly every American family can easily pass its family assets to their heirs with little or no estate tax due. Average Americans spend most of their time trying to manage their financial affairs for the week or the month. Some of them have the luxury of planning out for a year at a time. Few people have the time or luxury to lift their heads out of the weeds of their daily routine to think about long-term goals.

Chapter 3
Maslow's Hierarchy of Necks

"Dreams are often most profound when they seem the most crazy."
—Sigmund Freud

The giraffe has interesting symbolism and meaning in various spiritual cultures. The giraffe symbolizes grace, peace, individuality protection, communication, perception, and farsightedness. With its long neck reaching into the heavens, the giraffe symbolizes the ability to see the future and obtain things that would typically be out of reach. When your life is chaotic, the giraffe reminds you to keep your head up and avoid getting entangled in needless arguments. The giraffe appears to be both grounded and highly evolved at the same time.

These are prevalent characteristics of the most successful people I have worked with and interviewed for my books. Every one was confident enough to follow their vision and take significant risks. They were also able to remain grounded even after they achieved elevated levels of wealth, fame, and influence. The funny thing is that they were able to do it by "hacking" the traditional laws of psychology.

Normal Pathways of the Human Brain

Humans are not psychologically equipped to pursue higher levels of success. Abraham Maslow's hierarchy of needs came from his 1943 paper, "A Theory of Human Motivation," published in *Psychological Review*. With apologies to Maslow, we will simplify what human beings value, in order of importance:

1. Human survival: air, water, food, clothing, shelter
2. Safety and security: personal and financial, health, well-being
3. Social belonging: friendships, intimacy, family
4. Esteem: self-esteem, self-respect
5. Self-actualization: personal growth, development, full potential.

Maslow's Hierarchy

Self-actualization – You are living to your highest potential

Esteem – You've acquired skills that lead to honor & recognition

Love & Belonging – Achieving deeper, more meaningful relationships

Safety – Home, sweet home

Physiological Needs – Food, water, sleep

What this means is that people generally work from the bottom up in their emotional and psychological development. For example, if you don't have enough food, water or sleep, those needs will dominate your thoughts and actions. You would risk safety or love & belonging in order to find basic survival needs. Further, you would have a difficult time focusing on love and belonging in meaningful relationships if you didn't feel safe in your surroundings.

Successful People Are Psychotic

In Maslow's hierarchy of needs, the feeling of social belonging is right up there with love in his third level. People don't want to be alone—literally or figuratively. The only needs more imperative are our physiological needs—like air, water, food—and our need for safety. You could make a case that success leads to financial safety, but I am not sure that millions of years of evolution would support the purchase of a private airplane or courtside season tickets to calm a "fight or flight" reaction.

The reason we say successful people are psychotic is they don't suffer the same limitations in Maslow's model as other people do. In the introduction and first couple of chapters, you learned that super successful people achieve their success by being different. They stuck their necks out and did things that others did not do. The giraffes left the herd (more on this later) and did their own thing. In so doing, they often received criticism and sacrificed the 3rd level – Love & Belonging.

The most successful innovators, entrepreneurs, and trail blazers do not have that need that holds back so many others. They do not care about others' approval. They are comfortable going it alone as they find a new path to a place nobody has gone before them. This is a lonely existence, but it doesn't stop them from pursuing and achieving higher levels of self-esteem and self-actualization.

Charting a Better Path

If you want to successfully achieve or maintain a high level of affluence, you must be comfortable with your different circumstances and be comfortable doing things differently from your friends. If your only comfort comes from doing something and knowing that everyone else is doing it too, then you are destined to achieve and maintain mediocrity. The most successful people and families achieved affluence by being different and by doing things differently. If they did what everyone else did, they would be like 80 percent of Americans who earn less than $80,000 per year, and they wouldn't have achieved the wealth they now have.

Because the needs of this small group of high earners are so different from the bulk of our population, it's no surprise that they find it difficult to find good advice. The popular press, which is driven by its advertising revenue, must focus on delivering information that applies to the largest possible audience. The illustration of this point and its implication for the affluent *giraffe* is offered in the next chapter.

Chapter 4
Forget the Fox. What Did the Giraffe Say?

"What you do speaks so loudly that I cannot hear what you say."
—Ralph Waldo Emerson

Giraffes have enormous voice boxes, but nobody knows their sound. Are they speaking to each other at ranges the rest of us can't here? Is there a specific pitch or frequency that most people just can't identify, let alone decipher? That's their secret. Only another giraffe can truly know.

Not everyone understands everything that is said. From the giraffe, we should appreciate that maybe we can't hear (let alone understand) what a giraffe says because the message isn't meant for us. In the case of financial advice, it behooves you to "Be the Giraffe" to figure out which messages were intended for you and ignore the rest of them.

Most people believe there is more financial information available on television, in newspapers and magazines, and on the web, than one person could review in a lifetime. Six years ago, I thought that might be true. Now, I'm certain of it.

My Google search for "financial advice" on March 21, 2020 yielded 13.2 million results. For a previous book, I did the same Google search on June 23, 2014. Google gave me 2.67 million results. Do you believe 11 million useful pieces of financial advice have emerged in six years? It's impossible.

Perhaps searching for something more specific like "investing" would give us more targeted results. Hell No! Google returned 382 million search results (up from 50.3 million search results in 2014). When I tried to narrow the search to sites that had all of the following tags: "investing," "high net worth," and "financial planning." This narrowed the results to a much smaller, but still completely unmanageable, 300,000 webpages.

There are many places one can look for financial advice. Once you find seemingly relevant information, you have to ask yourself who is the intended audience. Consider the premise I made in a book I wrote for John Wiley in 2002. Most financial information available in newspapers, magazines, on television, or websites is inappropriate and often detrimental to successful financial planning for the affluent. This statement is even more accurate almost 20 years later.

How can there be so many places to find financial information, and so few reliable sources appropriate for the affluent? To answer this question, let's start by looking at a list of common sources of financial information. Which of these outlets would you consider appropriate for our high income and high net worth giraffes, and which would you consider to be directed at our zebra-like average Americans?

- Television: Fox News, MSNBC
- Newspapers: *New York Times, USA Today, Wall Street Journal*
- Web sites: FoxNews.com, CNN.com, CNNMoney.com, USAToday.com, WSJ.com, Forbes.com
- Magazines: *Smart Money, Money, BusinessWeek, Fortune*

This question above is rhetorical, but to stoke the fires of rhetoric, let's consider the income demographics of the audiences to whom these media are directed, as depicted in the table below (Remember that the median income for a family of four in the United States in 2017 was $63,030.).

Income demographics for various media sources.		
Source	**Type**	**Income Demographics**
Fox News	Television	$55,000.00 median HHI
MSNBC	Television	$54,000.00 median HHI
CNBC	Television	$63,000.00 median HHI
New York Times	Newspaper	$98,795.00 median HHI
USA Today	Newspaper	$91,683.00 median HHI
The Wall Street Journal	Newspaper	$257,100.00 avg. HHI ($2.616 million net worth)
FoxNews.com	Website	$70,000.00 median HHI
CNN.com	Website	$76,000.00 median HHI
CNNMoney.com	Website	$87,461.00 median HHI
USAToday.com	Website	$47,500.00 median HHI
online.wsj.com	Website	HHI >$100,000.00, 31.5% HHI >$150,000.00, 10.4%
Forbes.com	Website	HHI >$100,000.00, 41%
Fortune.com	Website	$78,000.00 median HHI
MarketWatch.com	Website	HHI >$100,000.00, 35.9%
Money	Magazine	HHI >$100,000.00, 44.6%
Business Week	Magazine	$154,346.00 median HHI
Fortune	Magazine	$90,596.00 median HHI

HHI, household income

Some of these popular sources of finance and other types of information appeal to readers of still lesser means:

Income demographics for various media sources.		
Source	**Type**	**Income Demographics**
ESPN	Television	$67,000.00 median HHI
The Los Angeles Times	Newspaper	$80,000.00 median HHI
LATimes.com	Website	$83,700.00 median HHI
ESPN.com	Website	$72,100.00 mean HHI
O (Oprah.com)	Website	$66,928.00 median HHI
People Magazine	Magazine	$67,757.00 median HHI
Sports Illustrated	Magazine	$69,509.00 median HHI
GQ	Magazine	HHI >$100,000.00, 37.0%
HHI, household income		

We are trying to illustrate with these data that almost all high-end magazines and websites in the first list have a typical audience with a household income of less than $100,000. Every outlet mentioned, except *The Wall Street Journal*, has an audience with an average household income of less than $155,000.

If you hold similar views as those of the colleagues and clients with whom we discussed these audiences, you would believe that almost all of the media mentioned above would deliver information targeting wealthier Americans. To compare the audiences of these information outlets, we went to each of their media kits and compiled the tables above in June 2014. You may be surprised the media outlets above focused almost exclusively on a non-affluent audience.

For the sake of argument, let's exclude *The Wall Street Journal* as an outlier. Our conclusion from the aforementioned data is that even the highest-level media outlets in the U.S. do not target and deliver content appropriate for an audience with an average income of more than $155,000. Let us explain why this is important to the discussion.

Media: Attract the Largest Possible Audience

If you are in the media business, it doesn't matter if you are publishing magazines, websites, producing television or radio programs. The goal is always the same if there is advertising involved—provide content that will generate a large enough audience to generate ad revenue. You generate ad revenue by proving that you can deliver a significant audience and accurately track the demographics of the audience.

All of the sites, magazines, and newspapers mentioned earlier are in business to make money. If they don't generate content that maintains an audience large enough to support the necessary advertising revenue, the company will go out of business. They must attract the largest audience possible.

The business model is that simple. To generate a large audience, these outlets have to deliver content that appeals to a broad niche of the American readership. After writing our last book, we appeared on more than 120 radio and television programs. Though the book, "Wealth Protection," had interesting philosophical lessons and more than 60 practical lessons on advanced financial, legal, and tax-saving techniques, nearly every producer and interviewer wanted us to discuss topics in the book that we thought were basic.

One host told us that his goal was to keep as many people interested as possible. He didn't care if the information was fresh and exciting. He wanted to make sure that "Joe Lunch-Bucket" (his words) wouldn't be put off by the discussion. He told us that talking about ways to save $100,000 in taxes, or ways to buy rental properties would alienate most listeners and would lose audience. He was not going to allow that to happen.

Until John Wiley asked us to write a book about affluent Americans, we had had very little interest from the popular press concerning the education we have regularly offered to high-income clients. Every information company is in business to make money. The money almost always comes from advertisers. Advertisers pay more if the audience is larger.

An information source must continually offer to the masses appropriate content to maintain and grow an audience and attract advertisers.

Charting a Better Path

Even the high-end distribution channels don't target consumers earning much more than $100,000. If you consider the five statements enumerated in this chapter, you can conclude that it is almost impossible for affluent Americans to find useful and appropriate financial information from popular newspapers, magazines, web sites, and television programs.

This is why most of the information contained in this book may seem foreign to many readers. The tips, tools, and strategies offered here are not the types of information that most information outlets would ever deliver because, quite frankly, there is no business reason for doing so. Roughly 10 to 20 percent of Americans will find the information in this book applicable and beneficial. If you prefer to place yourself near the top of this 10 percent, as you strive to have income and net worth similar to the top 1 percent or the top 0.1 percent, then this is the book for you.

Chapter 5
Giraffes Don't Want to "Fit in" with Any Herd

"I refuse to join any club that would have me as a member."
—Groucho Marx

Giraffes are non-migratory animals. They are free to roam wherever they desire. Though a group of giraffes may congregate in groups of up to a half dozen (in what is called a "Tower"), these groups do not generally form large herds. Their freedom of movement is not designated by other animals or impacted by the weather. Contrast that to the zebra, buffalo or wildebeest that form large herds and migrate following the rains — which give life to grasses they need to survive. The migrating animals make the epic annual journey across the plains and the dangerous rivers.

The giraffe has to make its momma happy and eat its greens, but it doesn't have to follow the rains. The giraffe eats leaves from trees with roots that extend 30 feet underground. Those trees can survive in areas without rain for years due to underwater aquifers. This nuance gives the giraffe greater freedom, flexibility and autonomy of motion compared to the millions of commuters who are slaves to traffic patterns.

Bernie "Zebra" Sanders for President?

The most successful outliers in any population understand that herds are the ultimate socialists. Every member of the herd shares in the bounty. Though this arrangement may be fair and equitable, the giraffes are willing to take some risk to do things differently – in hopes of a different outcome.

Giraffes represent the most successful and the most ambitious. These people don't want to "fit in." They believe in their intelligence, desire and drive and choose to bet on themselves. Despite the similarities they share as individuals with the masses, the giraffes understand the two groups have very different financial challenges that require different types of advisors and strategies. Giraffes don't need the financial and legal advisors that cater to the 150 million or so zebra. Giraffes don't need inexpensive off the shelf, low-cost solutions, or services. They want custom solutions that will help them stand out even further from those around them. Like zebra, giraffes can't help but talk about business and finance with their friends. A common characteristic of giraffes is that they don't need to brag about their planning or convince their friends to work with the same advisors to generate peace of mind. Giraffes cherish the novelty of being different.

They Lied – there is Danger in Numbers!

There is a secondary and hidden benefit the giraffe lifestyle offers. Herd animals stay in large groups for safety. They rely on "safety in numbers" which is a double-edge sword. Indeed, a group of predators will only take down one member of the herd at a time. Given there might be thousands, if not hundreds of thousands of potential targets in the plains at one time, you may like your odds. But remember the famous words of Lloyd Christmas in the movie *Dumb and Dumber*. When Jim Carrey's character asked Lauren Holly's character what the odds were of the two of them getting together, she said, "One in a million." His response was: "So you're saying there's a chance!"

This may seem silly. The movie is ridiculously clever and silly at the same time, it is also profound. As a member of a large herd, you are relying on safety in numbers, but there is guaranteed to be at least one death daily, and that could be you. Predators can, and do, easily find herds of hundreds, thousands, or even millions of animals. When a single animal leaves the herd, it is immediately targeted by the many predators following the herd. For that reason, once you are in, you can seemingly only leave for *your* last supper.

Though giraffes don't have protection from a herd, it isn't necessary. The giraffe avoids walking into a buffet by going places other animals are not. When they stumble across predators, it is usually an accidental encounter. By going where there aren't large groups of other prey, the giraffe increases its odd that it won't run into the lions and hyenas — or at least any healthy ones interested in hunting such large prey.

Counterintuitive: Big Word for a Silent Animal

The only way the affluent can achieve desired levels of wealth and have peace of mind is to follow advice that *doesn't* make common sense. Going against common sense is not easy. Many deeply rooted psychological factors push people to go with the crowd rather than against it—even in the financial planning context. As an example, consider this proposition:

It's a bad idea to pay off your mortgage and own your home outright.

For many of you reading this now, that statement may be difficult to accept. It is precisely the opposite of what your parents told you (and they are the smart people who taught you many life lessons). It contradicts the message of personal finance expert Suze Orman, and what hundreds of website and magazine articles and television programs suggest. Further, it just may not feel right, because it goes against what all of your friends are doing. Keep those feelings and thoughts in mind when you read the rest of this book.

Most children and adolescents try desperately to fit in. As we get older, we try to find the right groups in college. In our first jobs, we want to toe the company line. All states have laws that govern behavior. Most religions have commandments, rules, or other condoned and forbidden activities. Most people avoid actions they fear their friends and relatives would criticize. At the very least, most people refrain from sharing their potentially unpopular activities. We are not implying that Americans are sheep. Rather, we are saying that society typically rewards those who fit into the crowd and creates more challenges for those who do not.

While not a particularly astute observation, it is support for the significance of the number one challenge that must be overcome if you are to take advantage of the information in this book. To successfully take advantage of **gira*ffe*MONEY**, you have to do more than just admit that you want to be different. You must learn to embrace the fact that you *are* different.

Charting a Better Path

The difference between the very wealthy and moderately successful may be measured by income and net worth. More importantly, you now understand there are significant differences in how most successful people think, act, and feel about money. Their very different attitudes and methods of approaching wealth planning are integral to their success—these are their *psychographic* differences.

Along this path, you gained insight into why nearly every newspaper, financial website, and financial magazine is forced to focus its content on a group of subscribers or readers who have a very different set of concerns from the group you seek to become part of. These media outlets want to provide common-sense advice to the general public (zebra). This fits the business model of the popular media because there are many more zebra than giraffes – and the popular media are after the larger audience because it facilitates the sale of advertising space.

The most important lesson you saw along this path was to accept that you are different – and that you should look for different sources of information, guidance and motivation along your journey. Throughout the rest of **giraffeMONEY,** we will share a combination of financial lessons and psychological guidance you literally cannot get anywhere else. To prove this point, we invite you to move on to the 2nd Path of **giraffeMONEY** and combine your experience on playgrounds and in physics class to see how you can work less on your way to earning and building more.

2nd PATH
Stick Your Neck Out to Reach Higher

"I can't imagine why people are so unwilling to stick their necks out."
—Marie Antoinette

What do you know about giraffes? Giraffes have very long necks. The animal may be 20 feet tall, and the neck may represent more than 6 feet of that. Most people don't know that a giraffe has the same number of vertebrae in its neck as you and I do, which is seven.

Reaching heights of almost 20 feet, a giraffe can reach the tasty tree leaves that shorter migrating grass eaters can't even dream of having. As convenient as this is for the giraffe, it was not always the case. It's closest cousin, the okapi, is much shorter. Standing 5 feet tall, the okapi can eat shrubs, but not tree leaves. This amazing evolution for the giraffe took time. As it stuck its neck out further and further, it grew taller. The elevated perspective allowed the giraffe to see better paths and to reach the highest branches.

To get more of what we want, we have to leave the comfort of our couch. We have to stand up, stick our necks out, reach further, become comfortable being off-balance, and even risk falling. This lesson seemed to take as long for me as the giraffe's evolution. After delivering nearly 1,000 presentations over 20 years, a conference attendee told me he had been following me for years. When I asked him why he hadn't ever contacted me directly, he said, "I could never call you. You seem so unapproachable." Unapproachable? I was devastated. I hired a marketing, branding, and speaking team to help me figure this out. What I found was, being very smart reaches people at an intellectual level, but being very vulnerable touches people at their heart. Once I started writing and speaking about my shortfalls, failures, and insecurities, my speaking scores went up a little, but my personal and corporate engagements went through the roof. I also became happier and healthier – losing 30 pounds and increasing my income by hundreds of thousands of dollars per year while working 40 percent less.

The giraffe reminds us that everything we desire may not be right in front of us or within a comfortable distance. Only when we are willing to do what makes us uncomfortable will we reach those things that others won't. This is the premise behind www.GiraffeUniversity.com — an online learning community devoted to teaching new ways to look at helping entrepreneurs grow their companies, their cash, and their character. With separate pillars of personal finance, entrepreneurship, and transformation, GiraffeU offers videos, online trainings and live support to those who want to reach higher. If you finish this book and want more information, classes, programs, and tools in any of those areas, I invite you to join the GiraffeU community.

Along the prior Path, we observed that people acquire great wealth by doing things differently. No matter how different they are, the most successful have one thing in common. They all mastered the art of "Leverage." You will learn why leverage is so powerful, what types of leverage exist, and how to overcome limitations to increasing your leverage. You will see how successful investors have applied leverage to assets, credit, and even people on their way to elevated levels of wealth.

Chapter 6
Seesaw with a Giraffe?

"Nature is more like a seesaw than a crystal,
a never-ending conga line of bold moves and corrections."
—Diane Ackerman

Do you remember playing on a seesaw in the playground? The seesaw was the long plank balanced in the middle on a solid support (like a pole). I remember sitting on opposite sides with my younger brother. We would take turns pushing up from the ground with our feet. This simple game was fun for kids of relatively similar sizes, while secretly providing the foundation for physics lessons in science class. Without the fun of the static electricity generator, we will briefly revisit physics here.

I invite you to Google the word *leverage*. You will see links to the Cambridge English dictionary, Merriam-Webster dictionary, Investopedia, and thesauraus.com. You will find definitions of leverage as a noun and a verb. You will find both financial and business definitions.

One of Google's four definitions states:

lev·er·age *verb:* use (something) to maximum advantage.
"the organization needs to leverage its key resources"

Thesaurus.com offers a list of synonyms. I am partial to these three:

1) Influence
2) Advantage (or Edge)
3) Power

If you can influence others to help you gain an advantage or edge over your competition, you will have successfully achieved some level of power. Whether it was you or an older sibling, one of you had the power over the seesaw by leveraging greater weight – and I am sure it felt a lot better having the upper hand (and lower position on the seesaw).

You will even find technical and mechanical definitions that are inspirational – as you may want to see how much force you can exert on a screwdriver to your temple after reading them. One comprehensive, if not screwdriver-worthy, definition comes from BusinessDictionary.com:

> The ability to influence a system, or an environment, in a way that multiplies the outcome of one's efforts without a corresponding increase in the consumption of resources. In other words, leverage is the advantageous condition of having a relatively small amount of cost yield relatively high level of returns. See also financial leverage and operating leverage.

Leverage allows a person to be more efficient, more effective, and much more powerful. Leverage helps you get more done in less time, with less effort, and with less money. Do you know anyone who wants to spend more time and money while working even harder? If you are looking for a shortcut to financial success, leverage is the better path.

The Importance of Leverage

Earlier, you learned the differences between the middle to upper class of Americans and the group we refer to as "The Successful." This is the group of higher earners who have built significantly more wealth and influence than their peers. The Successful know that leverage is the single most important tool to building wealth. Without leverage, they would have to do everything themselves. They would have to run their own businesses and handle all of their financial affairs. They would pay for everything with only their own money and would micromanage the hell out of everything at work and at home. With those constraints, businesses and personal wealth would grow organically – at a snail's pace. If you resemble this remark, then you have not yet embraced the importance of leverage.

Leverage can make your life easier. You can use leverage to literally "buy time." By being more efficient, you will free yourself to do those things most important to you. Whether your current goal is maximizing your profitability, increasing enterprise value so you can sell your company, or finding time for the most enjoyable elements of life, leverage is your passport to *Successville*. Let's look at specific applications of leverage that I have learned from my most successful clients and colleagues.

Leverage Limitations

If some leverage is good, more leverage is better. Who wouldn't want to get more done with less effort or less money? The Successful have maximized leverage for thousands of years. It may seem like the amount of leverage one can attain is endless, but some rules that just can't be broken (not even by the most disruptive of us). Consider the following:

1. You only have so much energy.
2. You only have twenty-four hours in a day.
3. You only have so much money.
4. You can only borrow so much money.
5. You can only manage so many people.

When you reach the safe limits for each of these variables, you have reached your maximum capacity. You achieve efficiency by increasing leverage to a point where you approach your capacity without exceeding it.

Let's revisit the playground. You will get this lesson quickly if you had a bigger sister or brother, or a carelessly playful or sadistic parent. Remember what happened when the much heavier person got on the other end of the seesaw? The heavier person quickly sank to the ground – while simultaneously shooting you skyward on the other end. Only when they pushed up, would you temporarily go down. The heavier weight would ultimately bring their side back down to the ground – and allow them to control the speed and time of your play. At this point, it wasn't much fun. If you were afraid of heights like I was, it might have been a little scary for you too.

It is essential not to exceed your capacity. When you push too hard at one end, something is going to break. Your health, your marriage, or your relationship with your bank may suffer. When something breaks, you get to start all over again. Duplication of effort is not a sign of efficiency. Having to go back to start and retrace multiple steps is the opposite of leverage. It will severely deter your progress, if not derail you completely.

Charting a Better Path

When you understand that time, money and energy are all limited, you have to find ways to leverage them to get more out of life. This is true whether you are trying to grow your net worth, build your company, or increase your impact. As you ascend, you want to recall Icarus. Increase leverage without exceeding your capacity. Otherwise, you may fall and experience a catastrophe of your own. The 3rd Path will show you many ways to protect yourself from the mistakes that you are going to make, but that is not a license to work yourself to death or to scare away everyone from playing with you by pushing too hard. Leverage is about working smarter, not harder. For this reason, increasing effort is not leverage at all. Getting better results from less effort is the best way to achieve extraordinary levels of success.

Chapter 7
Make Money *Your* Slave

"When you combine ignorance and leverage,
you get some pretty interesting results."
—Warren Buffett

You understand that leverage is the key to working smarter, not harder. You also learned that having money helps you make more money. When you combine those two concepts, you get "Financial Leverage." The applications of financial leverage can help you change the way you think, work, and live, so you make money your slave – instead of the opposite.

Think about the most amazing sites you have ever seen. Which was most impressive? Was it the Coliseum in Rome, the Pyramids at Giza or possibly the Great Wall of China? Maybe it was one of the two tallest buildings in the world: 1) Burj Khalifa in Dubai or 2) the Shanghai Tower. It's okay if you were most impressed with Mall of the Americas. In each of these projects, levers are used in the construction. Whether they were using an ancient pulley system to construct the pyramids or a modern system of cranes to build a half-mile tall building, the most spectacular projects all required innovative uses of leverage.

Financial endeavors are similar to construction projects. The more ambitious the goal, there is a greater need for creative blueprints. That is only the beginning, as many people are needed to carry out the plans. In construction, there is a general contractor and scores of subcontractors. Financial planning is similar to construction in many ways. Someone has to be the architect of the plan that meets the client's goals and desires. Multiple specialists need to deliver expertise along the way. Somebody needs to oversee the process and make sure everything is working smoothly together. Unfortunately, this is much more the exception than the rule.

In working with thousands of professionals over the last twenty-plus years, this is the most significant difference in planning for giraffe clients. Most people work on their wealth part-time – when they aren't working in their businesses. Giraffes prioritize their wealth, hire extraordinary talent and pay them to run things by each other. This will be covered in the fifth secret, but it is important to review here, so you keep this in mind as you continue through the book.

Without exception, every multimillion-dollar earner and every $50 million family I know focuses on financial leverage as a key to success. Let's look at some specific ways they accomplish this.

Types of Financial Leverage

You can accomplish financial leverage by leveraging the two most valuable resources: time and money. When we talk about leveraging time, we are talking about limiting the amount of effort we must exert or patience we must have.

Buying Time. In previous books, I called this concept leveraging effort. I wrote that when I was in my twenties and pretty lazy. I thought the key was to get other people to do things for me. Though that concept is important (and covered in the fifth secret), it is not nearly as critical as saving time. There are many things we would all do *if we only had more hours in the day*. This is why leveraging "time" is integral for your success.

Consider how you acted when you were young. You may not have genuinely believed that you were immortal, but your behavior reflected otherwise. I remember college like it was yesterday, though my twenty-five-year reunion has already come and gone. We all remember driving fast, looking for all-you-can-eat buffets, and drinking cheap beer. Inexplicably, we bought the cheapest toilet paper because those precious few moments each day weren't worth the extra three cents. Hell, we thought pre-paying for a five-night stay in Las Vegas for the slightly lower rate was a great idea.

As we grew older, we gained that all too valuable elevated perspective. I turned forty-seven while writing this book. I know forty-seven is not that old, but I am closer to seventy than I am to my college graduation. That sucks. But, with age comes experience. We start to accept that we have less time. We realize the need to make smart choices – about our time, our friends and our health. When you have less time, you naturally become less patient. If you are unsure of that one, ask yourself if you have ever wondered, "Why does the microwave take so long to heat up this food?"

Still not convinced that impatience is setting in for you? Have you ever been on vacation, with no agenda, and felt agitated by the slow service?

It's not only slow food service that bugs us. We now have less patience for ignorance and stupidity. We have less patience with technology. We have less patience for everything – including financial success. Consider this real experience I had.

> **Education at 30,000 Feet**
> I once sat next to a senior executive from GE (General Electric) Capital. The man was in charge of healthcare acquisitions. At the time, I had just released my fifth book for physicians, and I was helping a couple of my doctor clients sell their patents and businesses. I remember what this man told me about GE's strategy for investing in (buying) businesses. He told me the largest company in the world was not buying your technology. It had the resources to figure out anything it wanted to figure out – including how to get around any patents you might have. When GE wrote you a check, it was buying time! By purchasing the technology, it was saving itself years of research and development so it could get to market before someone else did. This conversation left such an impression upon me that I am writing about it twelve years later.

There is a valuable lesson for all you smarty-pants out there. Regardless of your intelligence quotient (I.Q.), you only have so much time. That time may be best utilized closing the next deal, developing the next technology, or finding the next strategic partner. There is power in "smart partnering" so that you can save yourself the time it would require to "do it yourself." Along the 6th Path, you will learn how to get advisors in the insurance, investment, accounting and legal professions to work with you, instead of for you (or against you as many of you claim they do). When you structure your relationships and the engagements properly, you will save valuable time and effort – which will lead to making more money and is the next subcategory of leverage.

Making Money Work for You. Nothing is free. There's some sage wisdom for you right there. Seriously, every client I have ever had has always wished he or she had more money. It is not uncommon for an executive making one million dollars per year to balk at the buyout price of a competitor, or to hesitate to hire a superstar CFO who might cost 40 percent more than an average executive.

Even the two billionaires who recently hired me expressed cash flow concerns. One heavily invests in real estate resulting in lots of leverage restricting the family's ability to pursue some new ventures. The other was trying to build a foundation that would change the face of education in this country. Cash flow challenges limit their ability to do everything they want to do. I am not asking for violin players to step up and play a sad song for them. I am merely pointing out that we all have more dreams than we have resources to fund them.

This is the case with wealth. I refer to it here as making money, but it could easily be leveraging resources since wealth can be cash, securities, land, or business interests. In a world of commodity products like securities, real estate, loans, legal documents, and insurance, you would expect these products to be highly efficient. The services industries have managed to find a way to preserve significant fees and expenses in the products and services they offer in the upper end of town, where the clients are very busy and very successful. If you can save some of these fees and still receive extraordinary service, you can use that "found money" to fuel expansion plans or to fund your new ventures. These concepts will be discussed throughout and will be covered in greater detail along the 6th Path.

Leveraging Time *and* Money: Power of People

"We're all operating on borrowed time and borrowed money.
We need to make a choice."

—Douglas Rushkoff

When you leverage people, you can actually save yourself time and money. Giraffes know that leveraging other people's efforts is one way to get more than twenty-four hours of work done in a day. By leveraging people with special skills and expertise you don't possess, you can save yourself valuable time. By hiring lawyers, you get to skip three years of law school. We all see the doctor because we don't want to spend seven plus years in training and hundreds of thousands of dollars to be able to treat ourselves. Beware: leveraging people is a double-edged sword.

When you leverage other people to do certain tasks, you lose control of the process. If you don't hire the right people or put them into a structure that affords you optimal control and access, you may not get the outcome you want. Later in the book, you will learn how to structure entities that help align your goals and desires with those valuable people you will need to bring on board to achieve the leverage you require.

Charting a Better Path

Money is one of the ficklest mistresses (try saying that five times fast). Too many people spend their whole lives chasing it, failing to achieve any significant level of wealth because they are going about it the wrong way. They fail to utilize the three categories of leverage—leveraging effort, assets, and people. They also fail to leverage money itself. This leaves them a slave to the pursuit of money.

In the upcoming chapters, we will show you how to get more out of your time and effort so you can not only earn more, but also enjoy more of your success. We will then pivot into ways to protect your hard-earned wealth and move into more advanced ways to build a legacy and have a larger impact.

Chapter 8
Try Hard*ly*

"They say hard work never killed a man, but I say why take the chance."
—Ronald Reagan

Hard work is one key to success. You and I both know this from our own experiences. I try to explain it to my kids all the time – but they were never hungry a day in their lives, literally or figuratively. I fear this is one of those life lessons they will have to learn on their own.

Have you ever heard the phrase, "If you want to find a faster way to get a job done, give it to the laziest man?" The goal of this chapter on leverage is to help you get the most out of any level of effort. Whether you fancy yourself hard-working or lazy, leverage can help you get more out of your desired amount of effort.

In this chapter, we will discuss the capacity problems of leverage, how education can increase your ability to leverage your effort, and then suggest ways the Giraffes overcome the barriers of capacity.

Save the Hard Work Talk for Your Kids

The primary and inherent problem with effort is that you only have two hands and there are only twenty-four hours in a day. If we consider the case of two fishermen with very different work ethics, Slack Jack and Fresh Fred, we can illustrate these constraints.

> **Case study: Go Fish – Slack Jack and Fresh Fred.**
> Let's assume that Slack Jack and Fresh Fred earn $5 per pound of fish they bring in each week. Slack Jack works five days per week. He fishes for five hours per day and catches twenty pounds of fish per hour. If he brings in 100 pounds of fish per day, he will earn $2,500 per week before paying overhead, first mate, equipment, taxes, and so forth.
>
> Fresh Fred works six days per week, and he fishes for seven hours every day. He also catches twenty pounds

of fish per hour. Fred has little time off for family or hobbies, but he does earn $8,400 per week before expenses – which are considerably higher than Jack's because the first mate, gasoline, and bait aren't free.

Both of these fishermen might consider themselves successful (depending on their goals and values). However, if hard-working Fresh Fred wants to make more money, there aren't enough hours in the day or days in the week for him to make any more money unless he does something that earns him more money per hour or he finds a way to leverage something other than his own effort. Other applications of leverage could help Fred do just that.

Leveraging Education

The idea of leveraging education to create wealth is no secret. In fact, it has become part of the American Dream. For more than a century, immigrants have taken advantage of the U.S. and educational system. They have pushed their children to do well in school in the hope that the children would get good jobs and enjoy higher standards of living. They have also pushed their children to find careers that pay them more money than Fresh Fred's fishing business. This was eloquently and emotionally illustrated in Ramon Peralta's 2017 commencement speech to the University of Bridgeport's graduating class. Peralta shared the poignancy of his achievement, as the son of immigrant parents, and the first generation in his family to graduate from college. His story resonated with the families in the audience – many of whom were experiencing the American dream the same way his family had twenty-five years earlier.

Leveraging education is a key element of fortune-building and maintaining wealth. To prove this point, consider the following salaries of highly educated professions. When considering the earning potential of these professions, keep in mind the median household income (including the outliers) is approximately $62,000. Half of all United States households earned less than $62,000 per year. What education offers:

- The first-year salary plus signing bonus for an MBA (two years of graduate school) was $135,000 (www. http://managementconsulted.com).
- The median annual salary for a neurosurgeon in the U.S. was $609,201 in 2020 according to www.salary.com.

Neurosurgery requires completion of four years of medical school and a one-year internship as well as five to seven years of rigorous residency. You can see that leveraging education can help you earn more money per year and increase your wealth faster than if you have a job that requires a lower level of education, no matter how hard you work.

Education and Effort Are Not Enough

Would you be surprised to hear that the neurosurgeon mentioned above, and Larry, a landscaper who owns his own business have the same problem? While we are not saying that Larry the Landscaper is performing brain surgery, we are suggesting that they both have the same fundamental problem—albeit at a different level of income. Larry doesn't have enough hours in the day, or days in the week to increase his business beyond a certain limit. Similarly, a neurosurgeon's income is limited by the number of surgeries he can perform, which is also limited by the number of hours in a day, and days in a week.

Even if you assume that there is an endless supply of patients who need brain surgery and an endless supply of lawns to be mowed, both the landscaper earning $50 per hour and the neurosurgeon earning $500 per hour have the same capacity problem because:

1. They are limited in the amount of money they can earn until they figure out how to leverage what they do;
2. They only make money when they are actually working.

This lesson, the Giraffes figured out long ago. The secret to long term success is leverage. The keys to using leverage correctly are:

- Always focus on possible points of leverage in any business;
- Never consider increasing effort as a legitimate, long-term means to growth; and
- Never enter into a business that requires you to be involved in day-to-day operations.

For these reasons, we prefer to focus our articles, seminars, books, and personal consulting recommendations on strategies that help leverage assets *and* leverage people.

Charting a Better Path

Every teenager has parents, teachers, and coaches who tell them to work harder. I happen to be one of them, with three kids ages 12 to 18. Be a hypocrite like I am. Do as I do, not as I say (to them). Push your employees and children to work harder but know the secret deep in your heart. You have to work *smarter* without having to work *harder* if you want to reach those elevated levels of wealth. To see what that looks like, continue on your journey because the next two chapters share applications of this smarter-working lifestyle.

Chapter 9
Bust Your Assets

"It is much easier to put existing resources to better use than to develop resources where they do not exist."
—George Soros

Do you remember the phrase, "It takes money to make money," discussed in beginning of the book? The economic data supported the claim that having lots of disposable income contributes to exponential wealth accumulation. There are many valuable assets that you can leverage on your path to elevated wealth. These include:

1) Your money
2) Other people's money
3) Intellectual property
4) People

In this chapter, we will cover the first three. The next chapter, and the entire 6th Path are dedicated to the last item in this list. With nearly 8 billion people on the planet, you can appreciate the importance and opportunity of this one.

Leveraging Your Money

Leveraging your own money is the oldest and most basic form of leverage. It has been documented all the way back to ancient times of nations, empires, kings, and emperors. History demonstrates how nations had enough money to fund expeditions, to discover new lands, and acquire even more wealth. You can see the spoils of war with a visit to any of the museums in Rome, to the Tower of London, or to the more recently unearthed Liu Fei's tomb in Jiangsu, China.

Hundreds of years later, you can witness similar leverage used right here in the U.S. The Successful put their capital to work in various ways. If you have money, you can purchase land or real estate, and lease it to others who can't afford to buy the property outright. If you have excess money you don't need to spend to support your lifestyle, you can invest in long-term investments that have higher expected returns than shorter-term investments. These investments may be unavailable to others who require a short-term return to pay bills. Lastly, when you have money, you can use it as collateral to borrow new money, thereby using other's people money to make money. The Successful do this all the time to maximize wealth, which leads us to the next application of leverage.

Leveraging Other People's Money

Generally, using other people's money (OPM) is considered the classic definition of leverage. Using OPM as leverage often refers to credit, but we will broaden its definition to include all types of leverage involving OPM.

The most common way to use OPM is through debt. Many families have achieved wealth by borrowing at lower rates and investing the loan proceeds to achieve greater returns. This type of leverage is common practice among real estate investors. They put down a small percentage of the total cost to build properties and use OPM to fund the remainder of the costs. By borrowing money from the bank at rates that may be as low as 6 to 8 percent and developing properties that may have an overall return of 15 percent per year, the leverage gives the investor a significant return on his or her investment. Consider the following:

Financial Leverage in Real Estate Transactions			
Investor	**Amount Invested**	**Rate**	**Amount Earned**
Total	$10 million	15%	$1,150,000
Bank	$8 million	8%	$640,000
Developer	$2 million	25%	$510,000

Based on these numbers, the Developer can achieve a 25 percent return on his investment by using OPM leverage to fund a project he anticipates will yield a 15 percent total return. This is a classic example of how leverage works with real estate.

In other situations, such as starting a business, or making a speculative investment, the Successful can assume higher levels of risk because they don't need the money to pay for living expenses. This allows them to take chances and realize higher returns than less risky investments offer.

Another way to leverage OPM is called *equity*. That is, taking someone else's money, and giving them a piece of a business or investment in return. In this situation, the investor takes more risk, but also gets a higher expected return than the bank would get with debt. Although this kind of deal ultimately costs the Successful a larger portion of the total return, it doesn't have monthly or annual payment requirements the way a loan does. Giraffes enjoy greater short-term freedom with regard to cash flow because no interest or principal payments are due. In fact, even if there is a profit, the Successful may effectively borrow the investor's share simply by not distributing it and reinvesting in the next project.

Equity is best suited for deals that are more speculative, which cannot guarantee regular short-term income. Even well-established, publicly traded companies such as AT&T, Disney, Oracle, and so on, leverage equity occasionally. Many wealthy Americans have learned from these companies and offer equity positions to investors to fund the growth of family wealth, while offering participation in the upside.

Leveraging Intellectual Property

Since World War II, the most significant wealth accumulation has resulted from leveraging intellectual property. Intellectual property could be an idea, such as McDonald's fast-food assembly line concept, or technology that millions of people use, such as Facebook or Snapchat.

Other forms of intellectual property include copyrights on the Star Wars or Harry Potter stories. In these cases, an individual or a small group of partners develops an idea, proves it can work, legally protects the idea, and attempts to leverage it in ways that allow them to make money as a result of other people's efforts.

Consider three examples:

1. Bill Gates and Microsoft created the Windows operating system. Until recently, Microsoft didn't develop a desktop or laptop computer to run the operating system. Instead they created a system that would run on 95 percent of the computers in the world. Every computer that is built to run Windows results in a license fee to Microsoft. Gates didn't have to drive the increase in the sale of computers. Rather, he found a way to profit from the efforts of all the other companies that were building and selling computers, and from the software manufacturers that

were designing products to make the use of a computer a more enjoyable, and necessary, part of life.

2. The second example of a person who leveraged intellectual property is George Lucas. Lucas created the Star Wars concept. He made a few movies that became classics. However, the interest in the characters and story line didn't end with the movies. It expanded to action figures, lunch boxes, video games, and countless other items that were based on his concepts. Lucas could have tried the do-it–yourself technique, but that would have only yielded a fraction of the financial profit the leveraged approach achieved. Instead, he licensed his intellectual property to other people. Their efforts made Lucas hundreds of millions, if not billions, of dollars.
3. The last example of leveraging intellectual property is the McDonald's franchise of restaurants. One successful restaurant might have generated $100,000 to $250,000 of annual profit. An international chain of restaurants whose focus is on fast, consistently prepared food has served three billion customers and is worth billions of dollars.

My mother works with Conrad and Mark Wetterau. They would certainly be considered part of the Giraffe group. They own grocery stores, Budweiser distributors and Golden State Foods. Golden State Foods has 3,100 employees and is one of three facilities that process and package most of the food for McDonald's restaurants worldwide. Golden State Foods is an extraordinary facility with processes and controls that would blow your mind. Like the rest of the McDonald's system, Golden State Foods is an operation designed to create consistency and maximize leverage.

In less extreme cases, every city has a restaurant, dry cleaner, or other business that isn't particularly profitable on an individual basis. However, the owner may be able to take a unique approach, branding, experience or know-how and open additional locations and achieve a higher level of financial success. Many small business owners attempt to use leverage in this manner. Later, we will explore how publicly traded companies create much greater leverage through public markets, by buying private companies for a fraction of the value they will generate.

Charting a Better Path

Amateurs in the wealth accumulation game feel like they have made it when they earn enough to buy nice things. A beautiful home, luxury car, or expensive jewelry are all typical examples. The Giraffes do not look for things to buy. They look for places to invest. They do want assets that will help them generate additional wealth and allow them to buy accumulate more assets.

All three categories of leveraging assets—leveraging your own money, leveraging other people's money, or leveraging intellectual property—have proven to be very effective. Certainly, many have achieved super affluence by doing so. The important lesson is that you need to get the most out of your assets if you want to achieve a higher level of wealth. Now that you know how the affluent leverage assets, you are ready to learn the most powerful leverage technique—leveraging people.

Chapter 10
Call in the Cavalry

"The reason why a seesaw was made for two persons is that when you go down, there would always be someone there to lift you up again."

—Unknown

While leveraging assets is fundamental to wealth-building, you cannot achieve the highest levels of success without leveraging the efforts of other people. No matter how successful you are, you still only have 168 hours in your week. Every investment and each transaction requires people to manage it. As you become more successful, you will undoubtedly experience capacity problems.

No leverage discussion would be complete without mentioning the leverage of other people's time and energy. In fact, the leverage of people is so important to your success that we have broken it up into two sections. Here, you will learn the basic benefits of leveraging employees and advisors. In Chapter 29, you will learn very advanced methods of leveraging employees by transforming employment expenses into valuable long-term assets of your organization. Along the 6th Path, you will also learn how to more creatively structure relationships with your advisors, so they work better for you and your family.

Leveraging Employees – The Basics

The most common method of leveraging people is through hiring employees. Those with financial means can afford to hire other people to do jobs for them. The employer has successfully leveraged people if the collective group of employees helps the owner earn more money than the cost of the employee salaries and benefits.

The more employees you have, the more potential leverage opportunities exist. Sometimes you hire staff to support these employees. You hope the investment increases the productivity of the employees by more than the cost of the administrative support. To leverage your employees successfully and yield an increased profit, a simple rule is to pay people less than the value they provide your firm. Law firms have practiced this method for years.

For example, law firms may charge clients $200 per hour for an attorney's services and may require the attorneys to bill 2,000 hours per year. The firm collects $400,000 for the services of that attorney and may only spend $300,000 for that particular attorney's salary, benefits, and allocated overhead. The firm earns $100,000 per attorney.

If the firm can afford to hire ten, twenty, or 100 less experienced attorneys, and can find enough work to keep them busy, the senior partners of the firm can earn a very nice living—ten to twenty-five times that of average Americans, and five to ten times that of a less experienced attorney. In doing so, law firms are leveraging their employees productively. They train less-expensive attorneys to do the legal work, enabling the senior partners to land lucrative contracts and build valuable relationships for the firm.

In most circumstances, you don't get to "bill out" your employees which makes it much more difficult to quantify the financial return on a leveraged person. Often there may be equally important qualitative benefits, above and beyond the quantitative ones. Consider the benefits of leveraging employees as below:

1. By leveraging some employees, you can spend your time performing tasks that create greater profits. This is a quantifiable benefit. Using the example above, by having associates do the work, the law firm partners (also called "rainmakers") also do what they are best at doing: bringing in new business. Focusing on their strengths is likely a much more effective use of these attorneys' time. Stealing the thunder from the bestselling book, *The 4-Hour Work Week*, by Timothy Ferriss (Harmony, 2009) we want you to ask yourself: What is the best use of your time? Is it possible to pay someone to do the least profitable tasks you currently do? If so, you can take advantage of leverage.
2. By leveraging an employee, you can spend your time doing things you want to do. This is an important, but unquantifiable, benefit. If you could delegate employees to perform more of your work, perhaps you could spend time doing something you prefer to do, such as playing golf, spending time with family, or creating a new business that is closer to your passion. This is not financial leverage; it is emotional leverage. You can increase your

quality of life by using leverage to "buy time." What can be more important than that?

3. By leveraging experts, you are able to "rent" other people's expertise at a reduced cost. As we will see in the fifth secret, leveraging professionals is a cost-effective way allow you to spend your time working on profit-generating tasks and to "rent" the expertise of professional advisors. While it is possible that you could learn to become a CPA, money manager, and an attorney, learning these jobs would not be time well spent since you would only use this knowledge intermittently and it would take you away from things that are good uses of your time, skills and expertise.

Leveraging people who have specific expertise is economical. You can pay them less to help you than it would cost you (in time, money, and aggravation) to learn the skills and try to do the work yourself. Bill Gates didn't learn how to build computers and George Lucas didn't learn how to make action figures, instead they both benefited from someone else's expertise. Advanced, and potentially game changing, strategies for leveraging your employees are covered in the fifth secret. You will learn how to increase the profitability and sale value of your company, while building a team of dedicated, loyal, and hardworking employees who will act like owners!

Leveraging Advisors – The Basics

Leveraging advisors is absolutely integral to long-term financial success. Your epiphany will be when you realize that your time is worth more than your money. You should never spend your precious time on a task that could be done more efficiently and effectively by someone else. The importance of that statement is further amplified when the task in question requires special knowledge or experience. Consider the following case study:

Forget the Cobbler's Son.
Brain Surgeon Abuses Himself.
Nick the Neurosurgeon is massively underinsured. He has $30,000 per month of disability income insurance. His agent tells him that is all he can secure for him, even though Nick earns over $2,000,000 per year. Nick spends night after night researching disability insurance. He learns about personal policies and group policies. He explores ways to

> structure multi-physician associations and legal structures to increase his coverage. He eventually discovers that Lloyd's of London offers policies with limits in excess of $100,000 per month. He makes call after call to Lloyd's syndicates, only to find out that the he can't buy the policy directly.
>
> Nick eventually reads one of my physician-specific financial books and calls my office. I introduce him to a friend of mine, Dan Aceti. Dan is a disability specialist who has worked on executive disability solutions with Lloyd's of London for as long as I've known him. Dan was able to help Nick navigate the confusing policy language and the long list of complicating add-ons. In the end, Dan helped Nick avoid some of the more expensive policy terms that Nick mistakenly thought he needed to purchase. Ultimately, Dan secured a $100,000 per month disability income insurance policy for Nick.

Was this a success? Nick did get the policy he wanted, but he spent almost forty hours in independent and fruitless research. The equivalent of one week's work is worth about $40,000 to Nick. Nick would likely have enjoyed a week golfing on the beach, or with his kids, more than he enjoyed reading about disability income policies.

Insurance is a very common area of concern, where highly educated people insist on trying to do it themselves. This may be a result of the less-than-stellar reputation of insurance salespeople. For this reason, the 6th Path will show you how to eliminate the conflicts of interest in your insurance portfolio.

Mo' money, Mo' problems.

We have found the greater your success, the more complicated your situation. When your situation becomes more complicated, you will have a more difficult time keeping track of how changes in one area may influence other parts of your planning. To illustrate how complexity grows exponentially when you add more components, consider the number of relationships that exist in groups of various sizes:

How many personal relationships exist as groups grow?

Members in Group	Unique Relationships	List of Relationships
2 – Ann and Bob	1	Ann-Bob
3 – Ann, Bob, Chris	3	Ann-Bob, Ann-Chris, Bob-Chris
4 – Ann, Bob, Chris, Dave	6	Ann-Bob, Ann-Chris, Ann-Dave, Bob-Chris, Bob-Dave Chris-Dave
5 – Ann, Bob, Chris, Dave, Ed	10	Ann-Bob, Ann-Chris, Ann-Dave, Ann-Ed Bob-Chris, Bob-Dave, Bob-Ed Chris-Dave, Chris-Ed, Dave-Ed

The table above only considers direct relationship. You can appreciate that if something goes wrong with Ann's relationship with Bob, there may be an indirect impact on Ann or Bob's relationship with Chris or Dave. Similarly, business gets exponentially more complicated as you add people, business units, or areas of planning. You are going to need a great team of advisors to keep it all in line (or a healthy dose of morphine, so you just don't care if it isn't).

My situation isn't *that* complicated.

If you don't think you have complex goals already, consider the following partial list of common financial planning concerns. How many of these are important to you?

- Managing growth of your assets
- Managing lawsuit risks from employees, customers, competitors
- Protecting assets from eventual lawsuits
- Managing investment risk while attempting to grow assets
- Managing tax liabilities to maximize after-tax growth

- Managing business succession and estate-planning concerns
- Growing a business so you can sell it some day
- Protecting family members against premature death or disability
- Protecting inheritances against lawsuits, taxes, and divorce

If these are all on your "to do" list for this afternoon, this week, or this month, you are going to need that morphine mentioned in the previous paragraph. I am merely saying that the only way to handle these is by leveraging your team of advisors.

Charting a Better Path

We only have twenty-four hours in a day. We are limited in the amount of resources we can access at any given time. Limited time and money create our unique capacity. Leverage is not about working harder. You will be much better served to focus on working *smarter* without having to work *harder*. When we try too hard, or stretch our resources too far, we can suffer catastrophic setbacks.

The key to safely expanding capacity is through leverage. Leverage allows you to get more done with less effort, in less time, and for less money. Imagine "leverage" as the anti-child. Leverage gives you back everything that having children has zapped from you – more energy, more free time, and more disposable income. When was the last time you had too much of any of those?

You can't turn back time with leverage, but you can use leverage to make your time more valuable. You can leverage education to increase your earning potential (or that of your family members or employees). You learned the basic building blocks of leveraging employees and advisors to get things done for you. The advanced course will be offered in the fourth and fifth secrets.

You can leverage your money, other people's money and even your intellectual property to find ways to get more out of your assets, your people and your resources. Once you save money, you can reinvest to make more money or to create additional leverage. This is the compounding effect of leverage that the most successful giraffes have mastered.

With all your levers in place, you will be primed to make serious progress on your ambitious goals. When you are moving that fast, you are bound to make some mistakes. The next path will show you how to make sure that your educational experiences (others call them failures) will only be temporary setbacks on your road to elevated wealth.

3rd PATH
Don't Stumble into the Lion's Den… and Get Eaten!

"Even the straightest path has two directions."

— Paul McAuley, *Into Everywhere*

Like most wild animals in Africa, only a small percentage of newborn giraffes reach adulthood. When animals are small, they lack both the strength and the wisdom to avoid and evade would-be predators. This is certainly the case with a baby giraffe. Like all baby mammals, the giraffe needs to nurse and sleep (a lot) to grow. While nursing or sleeping in the grass, the baby giraffe can easily be taken by hyenas, wild dogs or a leopard — none of which are large enough to take down a fully-grown giraffe. With the help of its mother, and any other assisting adults in the area, some giraffes defy the odds and reach adulthood. At that point, the giraffe's life is less stressful, and it now has many choices of paths to take.

Can you see the similarities between a giraffe's journey and the first two paths to success? Along the first two paths, you had to become comfortable doing things differently from everyone else and you had to find ways to get other people to do some of the work for you —to become very successful. Given how counterintuitive both of those things are for most people, it's easy to see why so few people actually master the secrets of Giraffe Money and become very successful.

The similarities don't stop there. Once a majestic giraffe reaches upwards of 20 feet in height and weighs 4,500 pounds, it is not threatened by small predators or even a single lion. But that doesn't mean the giraffe is safe. Larger prides of lions, or smaller prides with multiple large males, can and do successfully hunt adult giraffes. If a giraffe is not careful to avoid lions it sees approaching, or it accidentally wanders into a lion's den, the opportunistic lions will try to end its life — and some attempts prevail.

It's natural selection when lions hunt other animals. The lions need to eat to survive. You should think about your business or your personal wealth as a giraffe. You defied the odds to get to where you are. You should be proud, like the majestic giraffe, but you can't become careless. Competitors and individuals with less than you have may see you as a target — that will allow them to survive or thrive if they take you down. When you consider that so few families acquire millions of dollars of wealth, you can appreciate why it's so troubling to me to see that success squandered because of carelessness, or as a result of an accident.

The focus of my first company, and many of my early books, was asset protection. During the height of the medical malpractice crisis, juries were awarding multi-million-dollar judgments and doctors' insurance rates skyrocketed. Over 10,000 doctors sought help from us in one way or another. When that litigation frenzy extended to people suing businesses, service providers, and even individuals, our practice expanded to include entrepreneurs and wealthy families.

In working with successful people, we found their fears extended to other concerns:

- Death or disability of breadwinner, partner, key employee;
- Economic downturns or disaster (coronavirus, 2020?);
- Threats (from outside businesses and inside employees);
- Divorce (of spouses, children, partners, or key employees);
- Accidental disinheritance; and
- Taxes

Just like the lions that can quickly end the giraffe's life, any of these threats could sneak up on you and destroy everything your family has accumulated. On this path, you will learn some clever ways to efficiently and effectively protect your family and your business from these (and other) threats. Keep in mind, there are many other ways to protect wealth beyond those referenced in this chapter. To supplement this section, see the comprehensive book, *The Giraffe Money Guide to Asset Protection*. You can find it at www.GiraffeUniversity.com/resources.

Chapter 11
Three Hyenas Walk into a Bar (Exam)

"He who is his own attorney has a fool for a client."

—Proverb

In Africa, hyenas are formidable predators. They have the strongest bite of any mammal, but that's not what makes them so vicious. Hyenas have the strongest stomachs — nothing makes them sick. They can completely digest bones, hooves, claws, and horns, and won't lose any sleep over it. When they are together in a clan, or a cackle, they are especially dangerous. They pick on, and steal, hard-earned kills from leopards and cheetahs. A large clan of hyenas will mob much larger lions and harass them into handing over their prizes as well. The combination of cunning, intelligence, and ruthlessness make hyenas extremely dangerous.

The single biggest threat to your business or your family wealth will be the hyenas you encounter on your path — lawyers! In the 1980s, the number of lawsuits in the U.S. skyrocketed, and large jury awards became commonplace. Whether lawsuits arise from employees or customers, distributors or suppliers, partners, or other owners, the direct and indirect costs of lawsuits are immeasurable. If you aren't careful, one lawsuit could destroy everything you have worked so hard to build.

The Lawsuit Explosion

According to courtstatistics.org, there were 83 million new lawsuits filed in State courts in 2017. That is one lawsuit for every 4 people in the United States. Is it possible that there is a 1 in 4 chance that you could be sued in any one year?

2017 Lawsuits Filed

State Court Filings	Trial Courts:	83,000,000 cases
	Appellate Courts:	241,000 cases
Federal Court Filings	District Courts:	354,000 cases
	Bankruptcy Courts:	789,000 cases
	Courts of Appeal:	52,000 cases

Source: courtstatistics.org

The Lawsuit Lottery

In our society, many people believe that misfortune is an opportunity to place blame and seek financial reparation—even if the target of the litigation was not at fault for the misfortune. Unfortunately, some juries have agreed that *someone* must pay for the alleged wrong doings. Through emotion and bias, juries sometimes award large sums of money to unfortunate victims, even when the defendants did nothing wrong, or the plaintiffs had some part in the situation themselves.

To illustrate this point, let's consider decisions reached in three cases:

Claim:	A woman sued a franchise eatery after being burned by hot coffee that she spilled on herself. She charged that the coffee was served at a dangerously high temperature.
Decision:	The woman received $2.6 million in damages.
Claim:	A trespasser was injured while burglarizing a home.
Decision:	The burglar received thousands of dollars in damages from the homeowner.
Claim:	A Pennsylvania woman sued a physician claiming to have lost her psychic powers during a routine set of tests.
Decision:	Woman received a jury award for $690,000. If her psychic powers were worth $690,000, how did she not see this loss coming? Maybe she did have psychic powers, which is why she sued him! You be the judge.

Potential litigants ask, "Why not me?" Press for these cases reinforces this belief. In turn, the number of people who try to use the system for personal gain increases, resulting in greater number of people who will eventually succeed. Each new outrageous success gains more press. The vicious cycle of lawsuits continues.

America is Already Great (for Attorneys)

Did you know that in virtually every other legal system in the world, a plaintiff who sues unsuccessfully has to pay the defendant's legal bills? This rule, called the *English Rule,* effectively prevents people from suing others unless they have a case with merit. If a plaintiff does not have a good case, he risks not only paying his own attorney's fees, but also those of the defendant.

This is obviously not the situation in the U.S. In most cases before U.S. courts, we follow thc *American Rule,* which dictates that each side pay its own legal fees, irrespective of the outcome of the case. This rule was originally created so that people wouldn't be discouraged from suing big businesses. Although the *American Rule* has merit, it created an entirely new profession – the contingency fee attorney.

As a plaintiff, you have a lot less to lose if you bring a meritless case. With the prevalence of contingency-fee attorneys, plaintiffs are literally in a no-lose situation because they risk nothing by initiating a lawsuit. Contingency-fee attorneys do not charge their clients hourly fees. Their only compensation is a percentage of the judgment awards in the cases that they win.

You Can't Blame Lawyers for Lawyering

Where there is smoke, there must be fire. The American Bar Association reported a total of 1,338,678 licensed, active attorneys in the United States. The total represents a 0.2 percent increase since 2017 and a 15.2 percent rise over the past decade in the number of U.S. lawyers. That means that one in every 248 people in this country are licensed attorneys. Dig deeper into the numbers and your will find that approximately one in every 150 Americans between the ages of 25 and 70 are practicing attorneys!

The top five areas with the largest number of active attorneys in residence are:

New York	177,035 attorneys
California	170,044 attorneys
Texas	90,485 attorneys
Florida	78,244 attorneys
Illinois	63,422 attorneys

New York tops the list with approximately one in every 70 adults is a licensed attorney.

With the increased number of attorneys in the population, and a societal shift from personal accountability toward placing the blame, it's no surprise that the number of lawsuits and bankruptcy petitions have skyrocketed in our country. A Giraffe will watch out for the hyenas and do everything in its power to avoid the dangers that surround them.

Beware a False Sense of Security

There are three very dangerous misconceptions that can lull you into a false sense of security.

Misconception #1: I already did my planning.

This is troublesome for three reasons. First, no plan is perfect. Most assets are protected differently under federal and state laws — and the variation in protections from state to state are significant. Further, only certain assets are afforded the ultimate levels of protection. Further, most strategies require ongoing maintenance that many clients and advisors fail to monitor — thus negating much of the protections. All of this is covered in great detail in the **giraffeMONEY** ***Guide to Asset Protection*** at www.GiraffeUniversity.com/resources.

Second, laws change. Even if you are an attorney specializing in asset protection, it is impossible to stay on top of all the cases and legislative changes that take place every year. There are federal laws, 50 different states, and multiple international jurisdictions to monitor. Any of these changes could destroy the protections of an existing plan or give you a very inexpensive alternative to your costly asset protection trust or international plan.

Third, you, your business, and your family change. This doesn't mean that you don't value protection. Your business structure may have changed. Your assets may have grown considerably. Your children may be married (and you don't want them to lose an inheritance to divorce). Perhaps you now have grandchildren and you'd like to leave more to them than to your children, who are already successful. Every family's wishes change over time — and they outgrow older plans.

Misconception #2: I Don't (or Won't) Own Any Assets
Most people hold their homes and other property in joint ownership or in their living trusts. Unfortunately, neither of these ownership structures provides much asset protection in either community property or non-community property states. Some people like the idea of putting assets into a spouse's or child's name to protect them from creditors. If the assets were not properly transferred and gift tax returns filed, these types of transferred can be subject to significant gift taxes (plus interest and penalties). Transfers performed after the event that ultimately resulted in liability can be deemed to be "fraudulent transfers" and the transfer can be reversed. You don't have to know that you did anything wrong, let alone be warned of a lawsuit, to be guilty of committing a fraudulent transfer.

Misconception #3: I Am Insured, so I'm Covered.
I can't argue over having insurance but realize that an insurance policy is 50-100 pages long for a reason. There are a variety of exclusions and limitations that most people never take the time to read or understand. Even if you do have insurance, and the policy does cover the risk in question, there are still risks of underinsurance, strict liability, and bankruptcy of the insurance company. If you are uncertain that these risks are significant, as the former president of a reinsurance company and a co-founder of a captive management company, I helped hundreds of business owners create and manage their own insurance companies to handle risks that were uninsured or underinsured through traditional insurance policies. In many cases, these business owners identified risks that warranted annual premiums of upwards of one million dollars or more. Don't be misled to believe that every risk in your business and to your family will be covered by insurance. The policies you have are long legal contracts with numerous exclusions to protect the insurance companies' interests – not yours. It's better to be safe than sorry.

Charting a Better Path

At this point, we hope you realize what giraffes already know. It is too difficult to become successful only to allow someone else take it because of carelessness. You have to spend as much time preserving what you have as you spent acquiring and growing it. Money spent on proper legal structuring can provide invaluable protection from lawsuits. Along the 2nd Path, you learned that giraffes are keen students of leverage — they love implementing strategies that offer multiple benefits. As you continue on your journey through this book, you will see that many of the same strategies that protect your assets and your future income from lawsuits also help you reduce unnecessary taxes and increase the overall value of your family wealth.

To learn how best to do this, you can read the much more detailed information in the special report **giraffeMONEY** ***Guide to Asset Protection*** available at www.GiraffeUniversity.com/resources. Now, continue down your path to see what other threats giraffes protect themselves from on their way to increased wealth and greater happiness.

Chapter 12
Master Social Distancing: Get and Stay Ahead

"It is far better to be alone, than to be in bad company."
—George Washington

Giraffes are non-migratory. They are solitary, yet social, creatures that do not form lifetime herds like almost all other herbivores. Giraffes will create small groups, or Towers (one of the coolest group names in the animal kingdom), for specific reasons. Towers may form to attract a bull male for mating, for protection of newborns, to provide protection in a dangerous area, or for temporary social interaction. Individual giraffes seek the benefits of the group during these short stints, but they do not trust their future to the vision of another. After some time, each of these giraffes goes its own way. Giraffes enjoy temporary affiliations but remain independent.

This is an important lesson for businesses and families that want to maximize the value of their overall assets while preserving each business unit, asset, or personal holding. The key to asset protection is to divide assets in ways that add value to the total enterprise, without sacrificing the value of any one asset. Let's explore this more closely in the context of a business and then, we can look at the modifications for a family.

Danger is Right Under Your Nose

I know that starting and running a business is difficult. I have started ten, and only successfully sold two of them. With so much on any business owner's plate, we all seek as much simplicity as possible — because we know that leverage is important, and our time is the most valuable asset we have. Unfortunately, in our attempts to simplify, we often make it easier for hyenas to attack and damage us.

Would you believe that most businesses who hire me have maximum lawsuit exposure? Ask yourself these questions:

- Is your equipment or real estate owned by you personally?
- Is your equipment or real estate owned by your operating business?
- Are your lease or key business contracts executed with your operating business?

If you answered "yes" to any of these questions, your business is vulnerable. This is only the beginning of the lawsuit risk quiz. Consider the following questions:

- Do you have an employee manual that has been reviewed and updated recently?
- Is your retirement and benefits plan compliant with recent federal law changes?
- Have all employees signed valid non-compete and non-disclosure agreements?

If you answered "no" to any of these questions, you and your business are vulnerable to financial risk. The more comprehensive solutions can be reviewed in the **giraffeMONEY** ***Guide to Asset Protection*** available at www.GiraffeUniversity.com/resources.

Step 1: Segregate Assets to Keep Business Going

Along this path, you may have noticed:

1. There is a need to protect assets in our highly litigious society.
2. Very little asset protection is offered by conventional wisdom in financial planning.
3. As a business owner or real estate investor, you have significantly more to lose.

We all learned something about social distancing in 2020. By limiting interactions, we can reduce the possible spread of a deadly virus. This is the same theory behind using asset segregation to separate assets and value from an operating business. There are two reasons to separate the ownership of real estate, assets and equipment (RA&E) from the operating business. First, the RA&E are valuable assets that should be isolated from any liability created by the business. If your business has a lawsuit from a customer, employee, or vendor, a future judgment against the company would put all of those valuable assets at risk.

Second, some of your corporate assets could generate their own liability. In the case of real estate, that liability could show up in the form of *slip-and-fall* claims from people coming and going on the premises. If your business owns cars, trucks, planes or helicopters, the operation or negligence in maintenance could result in injuries or death (see Kobe Bryant's death for an example of such a lawsuit).

When the operating business owns all of the assets within the same legal entity, you risk cross contamination. With "all the eggs in the same basket," one mistake or unfortunate event could result in complete financial ruin. What is the alternative? Asset Segregation.

4-Step Plan to Protecting Your Business

Step 1: Identify which of your business operations could generate liability. Usually, this includes any contractual relationships – such as employees, customers, vendors, and distributors – that could result in a lawsuit.

Step 2: Identify which business assets are "safe" and which are "dangerous." A safe asset is one that is valuable to your company and highly unlikely to generate any liability. These include inventory, cash, goodwill, leases, contracts, and intellectual property (copyrights, trademarks, patents, and customer lists). A dangerous asset is one that could be the source of liability. Real estate could result in a variety of premises liabilities. Products that are manufactured then sold or leased, could result in lawsuits as well.

Step 3: Create new legal entities that offer protection such as limited liability companies (LLCs), Family Limited Partnerships (FLPs) or special types of irrevocable trusts. How and why these entities are so much safer than corporations is outside the scope of this book, but are described in great detail in **giraffeMONEY** ***Guide to Asset Protection*** available at www.GiraffeUniversity.com/resources.

Step 4: Segregate the ownership of valuable assets from both operations and from assets that may generate liability. When you do this, you limit the impact an unfortunate event or overzealous plaintiff can have on your business. More advanced business owners can layer in advanced estate planning and tax-savings techniques to reduce hundreds of thousands, or millions, of dollars in unnecessary payments.

The Better Way to Own Assets in Your Business

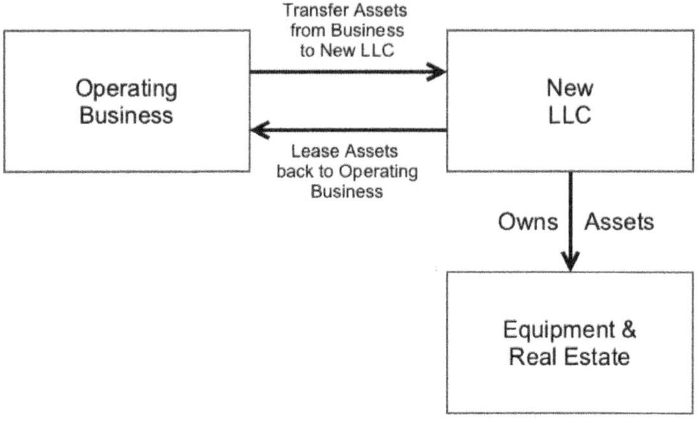

Step 2: Think of your Family as a Business

You can separate corporate assets from the operating business, but you may be wondering how to separate family assets from the family. You first have to avoid making common mistakes. Investments should never be owned in your own name, jointly with a spouse, or in your living trust. These ownership structures provide little to no protection from creditors. You should consider using combinations of limited liability companies (LLC) and special trusts (see Chapter 22 for my favorite form of asset protection) to own family assets in ways that protect them from lawsuits, unnecessary taxes, and even divorce. For a more comprehensive review of personal asset protection tools and strategies, download the **giraffeMONEY** *Guide to Asset Protection* at www.GiraffeUniversity.com/resources today.

Charting a Better Path

Giraffes enjoy freedom on multiple levels because they do not restrict themselves to following a large herd. The primary benefit of a non-migratory lifestyle is freedom of choice. Giraffes may pursue their own paths — instead of following the endless cycle of migration that is dictated by rains. The secondary, and very attractive, feature of being away from a herd is the freedom of movement. Despite the fact that the giraffe is so large, it often is not noticed by predators. The giant giraffe often goes unnoticed or ignored because lions are attracted to the irresistible sounds and smells of the million members of the migrating buffet.

Don't be like the many business owners who look a lot like zebra. They have their heads in the weeds all day, focusing on making money, until danger is too close to avoid. They think there is safety in numbers, but the reality is that wealth and success attract predators who would like to take what is yours. Be proactive and protect your business and personal assets by segregating them using asset protected legal structures and financial instruments. By applying the rules of social distancing to your assets and income sources, you can limit the potential spread of a financial or litigation threat.

Chapter 13
Don't Let Death Be Contagious

"I'm always relieved when someone is delivering a eulogy and I realize that I'm listening to it."

—George Carlin

This chapter is not about some rare disease or virus that infects only giraffes and spreads across the entire species. The important observation to make along the path is that one unfortunate event does not have to impact everyone associated with it. More specifically, a premature death doesn't have to be emotionally *and* financially devastating to a family or business.

Don't Bet Your Life

The emotional distress caused by the premature death of a loved one cannot be exaggerated. However, long before the psychological scars begin to heal, financial devastation may begin for surviving family members.

When families fail to purchase enough insurance to replace the income of the deceased or to pay the taxes and other liabilities due at passing, it is usually because they failed to execute an obvious plan. Spouses are well aware of the contributions each is bringing to the family. Both are very well aware of the outstanding liabilities — mortgages, loans, future college tuition, weddings, etc. There is no explanation for not having enough insurance on each spouse — except that they lost their gamble. They wanted to spend the money on other things and, before they got around to buying the life insurance, something bad happened.

According to the U.S. Centers for Disease Control and Prevention's most recent data, stroke killed nearly 130,000 of the more than 800,000 people who suffered one. Other statistics in regard to types of unforeseen death include:

- In 2006, an American had a one in 19 chance (5.26%) of dying as a result of a stroke.
- Stroke was the third leading cause of death in 2009, the most recent year for which statistics are available.

- Accidents accounted for 113,000 deaths in 2005 according to the most recent statistics available from the National Safety Council.
- Accident was the number five leading cause of death in the U.S. and the number one cause of death among people aged one to 41 years of age. Accidental death is increasing in rate much more quickly than the four other leading causes of death: heart disease, cancer, stroke and chronic lower respiratory disease.

In addition, a number of people will discover they are terminally ill, and their families will no longer be able to purchase personal life insurance to help them manage the financial burden created when they pass away.

How Much Life Insurance Does a Family Need?

The first financial effect of death, especially for younger families, is the lost income. If the family hasn't met all of its saving goals (most don't until the income earners are well into their 50s), the death will result in a significant financial strain. The key to maintaining wealth is making sure that no financial catastrophe wipes out the family assets. I have saved you the hassle of doing the math, but consider the following:

- The present value of 20 years of lost income for the average American family (with $60,000 of annual income) is approximately $848,000. That means that, at the time of death, the family would be in the same financial situation if they had 20 years of income or had a lump sum of $848,000.
- For a breadwinner earning $150,000 per year, the present value of 20 years of lost income is more than $2.1 million.
- If you earn $400,000 per year, the present value of future income is $5,600,000.

What these examples illustrate is that a family needs life insurance in the amount of at least 14 times the annual income of each wage earner, just to keep them on track to meet their financial goals (assuming that their current earnings were keeping them on track). Also, this estimate assumes no adjustment for inflation. As such, the savvy buyer typically purchases life insurance in the neighborhood of 20 to 25 times income in order to avoid financial disaster and to protect the future income for their families.

Prepaid Aggravation Insurance

In addition to replacing income, the savvy giraffes want to eliminate unnecessary headaches for their heirs. This is less about having people profit from your death, and more about realizing that the emotional impact of losing a family member may lead to some difficulties managing the family finances. This was the case for my mother after my stepfather passed away in 1988 (in his early 40s). She ultimately lost her home, then was forced to file bankruptcy.

Aggravation, or headache insurance is about paying off debts. These include any potential estate taxes or state inheritance taxes, outstanding mortgages and loans, unfunded college savings plans, and any weddings or other promises to children. The total amount will differ for each family, based on the total amount of outstanding mortgages and business loans, thc number of college-bound kids, and irrational daughters who insist on getting married. Add this total amount to the income replacement amount above to arrive at your target insurance amount.

How Much Life Insurance for a Business?

Like many things in life, there are "needs" and there are "wants." This is particularly true of life insurance in the business context. Along the 6th Path, we will share advanced strategies for maximizing the value of a company, minimizing tax liabilities, and reducing the costs of transferring a business or family fortune. Many of these strategies will utilize insurance as part of the planning, but they are growth techniques. Since we are on the 3rd Path showing you how to protect yourself and your business, we will only discuss the three categories of insurance you "need" to continue your business:

> **#1 Very Rainy-Day Fund.** In the event that the owner, president or key player dies, a business could suffer in various ways. Banks may suspend lines of credit. Customers or distributors may suspend orders (and payments). Clients may fire the company. It is important for a company to have access to three to six months of working capital to get through this uncertain time.
>
> **#2 Key Person Replacement Fund**. When an owner or key employee dies, the impact on the business could be considerable. The Very Rainy-Day fund will keep the

company in operation, but that isn't enough. You have to recruit, hire and train the replacement. This can often cost twice the annual salary of the person being replaced.

#3 Buy-Sell Agreement Fund. When an owner dies, the business or the other owners will want to buy the shares of the company from the surviving spouse, child or heir. Otherwise, the business will have to deal with a new owner who may not have the training or experience for the job. On top of that, this person will be in a highly emotional state. These are not the traits you are looking for in a partner. You need to carry enough life insurance (and lump sum disability insurance – #foreshadow) on each of your partners to buy out the owners' survivors.

Charting a Better Path

When you add up the different categories in the family column and the three categories in the business section, you will come up with the total death benefit you need for each family member, each owner, and each key employee. Later in the book and at GiraffeUniversity.com, you will learn how to use leverage to obtain this insurance cost effectively such as buying discount coverage for groups and using other people's money to pay for the insurance you need and want.

Of all the threats you face, death is obviously the most permanent. There is a less permanent, but far more destructive risk facing you and every person in your business. It could be more economically devasting than death. Continue on your path to uncover this hidden threat and learn how to protect yourself.

Chapter 14
A Fate Worse than Death? Financially, Yes.

"If stupidity were a disability,
I know some people that would get a monthly check."
—Unknown

Unless you have sold your company, received a huge inheritance, or are retired, your single greatest asset is likely to be your earning potential. While most people are underinsured, they do have at least some life insurance. However, most professionals, business owners, and executives completely overlook a more statistically dangerous threat to their long-term financial stability—their own disability.

What is the risk that the average individual will suffer a disability? According to the Council for Disability Awareness, Personal Disability Quotient calculator (www.disabilitycanhappen.org/chances_disability/pdq.asp.):

- A healthy 35-year-old female that is 5'4", 125 pounds, and a non-smoker, who works mostly an office job, with some outdoor physical responsibilities, has a:
    - 24 percent chance of becoming disabled for three months or longer during her career;
    - 38 percent chance that the disability would last five years or longer;
    - If this same person used tobacco and weighed 160 pounds, the risk would increase to a 41 percent chance of becoming disabled for three months or longer.
- A healthy 35-year-old male that is 5'10", 170 pounds, and a non-smoker, who works mostly an office job, with some outdoor physical responsibilities, has a:
    - 21 percent chance of becoming disabled for three months or longer during his career;
    - 38 percent chance that the disability would last five years or longer;

- If this same person used tobacco and weighed 210 pounds, the risk would increase to a 45 percent chance of becoming disabled for three months or longer.

Why do I say that inadequate disability income insurance coverage can be more costly than death? In both cases, the breadwinner will be unable to provide income for the family. However, in the case of death, the deceased earner is no longer an expense to the family and may, through life insurance, leave a liquid asset at death. If the breadwinner suddenly becomes disabled, that individual still needs to be fed, clothed, and cared for by medical professionals or family members. In many cases, the medical care alone can cost hundreds of dollars per day – and the life insurance death benefits do not pay out. With a disability, income is reduced or eliminated, and expenses increase. This can be a devastating turn of events and can lead to creditor problems and even bankruptcy. Let's look at how we can protect ourselves from this major threat.

Not Having Disability Hurts – Know, Know, Know!

No one ever plans on becoming disabled—although half of us will experience a long-term disability at least once in our lives. Just because you had one disability doesn't mean you have a get out of jail free card for the rest of your career. I have been disabled three times – and I'm not even 50 yet! I missed 120 days of work in 1995 when I ruptured a disk playing basketball, and another 60 days when I tore my Achilles tendon (playing basketball, again) in 2014. Despite my retirement from basketball after the Achilles tear, I missed another 60 days in 2017 when I had spine surgery. I would love to assure you that I took my lumps so you won't have to, but the odds are either you or your spouse will experience at least one disability in your career. Though disability insurance may seem like a boring topic compared with some of the more exotic material in the book, this may be the single most important lesson you learn.

Getting the Best Coverage for the Money

You need to know what to look for to get the best coverage available, at a reasonable price. The following questions are important for you to ask when considering a disability policy.

What is the benefit amount? Most policies are capped at benefit amounts that equal 60 percent of the disabled person's income. Some states and insurance companies have monthly maximums as well. Ask yourself how much money your family would need if you were to become disabled. Even though most traditional insurers offer maximums of $7,500 or $10,000 monthly, there are specialized channels (like Lloyd's of London) where we have been able to secure $5,000 to $50,000 additional monthly coverage.

What is the waiting period? The waiting period is the period of time that you must be disabled before the insurance company will pay you disability benefits. The longer the waiting period before benefits kick in, the less your premium will be. Essentially, the waiting period serves as a "time" deductible. With health insurance, you cover the first costs out-of-pocket up to a specified limit (your dollar deductible). With disability insurance, you cover your expenses for the waiting period, then the insurance company steps in to help. If you have adequate sick leave, short-term disability, an emergency fund, and can support a longer waiting period, choose a policy with a longer waiting period to save money.

How long will coverage last? Be aware that many policies cover you for only two to five years. Unless you are 60 to 63 years old, this would be an inadequate. If you can afford it, look for coverage to age 65. Unless you are so young that you haven't yet had time to qualify for Social Security, a policy that provides lifetime benefits, at costly premiums, is generally not worth the added expense.

What is the definition of disability in your policy? The main categories are *own-occupation, any-occupation,* and *loss of income.* The own-occupation policies, which pay a benefit if you can't continue your own occupation (even if you can and do work another occupation after the disability), are the most comprehensive, and the most expensive. Two important elements to look for in an own-occupation policy are:

1. Are you forced to go back to work in another occupation?
2. Will you receive a partial benefit if you go back to work slowly after the disability, and make less than you did before the disability?

Does the policy offer partial benefits? If you are able to work only part-time instead of your previous full-time hours, will you receive benefits? Unless your policy states that you are entitled to partial benefits, you won't receive anything unless you are completely unable to work. Are extended partial benefits paid if you go back to work and suffer a reduction in income because you cannot keep up the same rigorous schedule you did before you were disabled?

Important note: Partial benefits may be added on as a rider in some policies and should be seriously considered as only three percent of all disabilities are total disabilities.

Is business overhead expense covered? When you go into business on your own, the last thing you think about is not being able to pay your bills. Even if you have $10,000 or $20,000 of monthly disability benefit, you likely don't have enough to cover your lost income *and* the costs of running your business. Many carriers offer up to $25,000 or more per month to cover business overhead expenses.

Is your policy non-cancellable or guaranteed renewable? The difference between these two terms—*non-cancellable* and *guaranteed renewable*—is very important. If a policy is *non-cancellable,* you will pay a fixed premium throughout the contract term. Your premium will not go up for the term of the contract. If it is *guaranteed renewable,* it means you cannot be cancelled, but your premiums could go up. As long as non-cancellable is in the description of the policy, you are in good shape.

Other issues to consider when determining if you are getting the best disability insurance coverage for your money include:

- Increased coverage
- Cost-of-living increases
- Waiver-of-premium
- Return-of-premium waiver
- Unisex pricing
- HIV rider
- Multi-life pricing discounts
- Protection of future pension contributions

Disability of a Business Partner

The disability of a business partner can be just as financially crippling as the disability of the family breadwinner. There is a strong financial tie between business partners and there may be an even stronger financial dependency between business partners than exists between spouses. When a partner becomes disabled, the business will lose significant revenue while possibly facing increased costs to replace the disabled partner. The end result could be financial devastation for the remaining partner and the business without a buy-sell agreement tied to disability income insurance, with a lump sum payout to generate funds to buy out the disabled partner.

Charting a Better Path

The likelihood of a disability is greater than the probabilities of a premature death, a lawsuit, and a bankruptcy combined. Giraffes know that disability income insurance is the only way to keep them up and moving along the path – and continuing to earn income. This is the most overlooked coverage I see with business owners, and I cannot overstate the importance of having a comprehensive disability policy as part of any personal financial plan. This policy is an integral funding mechanism for a buy-sell agreement for disability of a business partner which is covered in the next chapter.

GiraffeU has partnered with one of the leading specialty disability income insurance organizations in the country to provide free analyses of your existing disability for employees, executives and owners. If you would like a take advantage of this free offer, please email us at: benefits@GiraffeUniversity.com. One of our team will contact you within 48 hours to help you collect the necessary data required for this analysis.

Chapter 15
Pretend to Be an Elephant – Don't Forget This One Thing

"Not only is my short-term memory horrible,
but so is my short-term memory."
—I forgot who said this

Imagine a giraffe galloping at 20 to 25 miles per hour down a path. However, instead of leaning forward and looking ahead, picture its neck is twisted around so the giraffe can look back at what may, or may not, be chasing it. This is what risk management and asset protection feels like to many business owners. Why? Consider that most successful entrepreneurs are optimists. In the wake of risks and worries that keep others from risking everything and trying the impossible, "giraffes" go after it 10 to 12 hours per day, six or seven days per week. I know, because I have walked that path for nearly 25 years. Abandoning big picture ideas and grandiose achievements to contemplate all the things that could go wrong feels like a betrayal of our DNA.

Always Expect the Unexpected

We can't predict how life will work out for any of us. We certainly can't predict exactly how a new business will go. But I *can* predict one thing about any business that has multiple owners – it won't last. I am not saying that two or more people can't successfully work together in business. I am saying that multiple people will not remain partners forever.

When the partners attempt to unwind what they have created, those who ignored the most fundamental legal contract may jeopardize all of their hard work. This very important legal contract is the *buy-sell agreement.* This agreement, signed by all owners, outlines how the business will be valued at the time of one partner's death, disability, or disagreement with the other partners. It also explains how the purchase of the departing partner's shares will be paid.

Without a buy-sell agreement, partners and surviving family have no legally enforceable plan. At a time when the family is grieving, and possibly struggling to pay its bills, members of that family will look to the surviving partners' business for help. At the same time, the surviving partners may be struggling to get by without the services of a valuable owner. The last thing either of these two groups need is a power struggle over money. In too many cases, the absence of a buy-sell agreement at the time of death can cause bankruptcies of the families, or a forced sale (at a below-market price) of the business.

If you are unsure what life might look like if you don't have an executed buy-sell agreement, every partner in your business should ask him/herself these questions:

- What happens if and when any of my partners die? How will their families fare as owners of my company? Do I want them as new partners? Could I afford to buy them out?
- What happens to my share of the business if I decide to exit the business or decide to retire? Would my partners be mad? How could I ensure they would give me my fair share?
- What happens if any of my partners become disabled? Would I want to pay them their percentage of earnings even if they didn't come to work? Would I be willing to kick them out of the business when they were hurt?
- What happens if any of my partners have ugly divorces? Would I want their vengeful ex-spouses as my new partners? Would I have the money to buy them out? Would they even accept my offer if they weren't obligated to take it?
- What happens to my family if I die or become disabled? How will I know they will receive their fair share of the business? Can I trust my partners and their spouses to want to take care of my family?

As you can see, there are many potential pitfalls if you don't create a contractual obligation for all partners using a properly executed buy-sell agreement.

Let's look at the case study of Fred and Barney involving only one of the many areas where a buy-sell agreement has great utility. As you'll see, their story of a two-person firm losing one partner is a typical case.

> **Case Study: Fred and Barney**
> Fred and Barney are owners of a $10 million (annual revenue) rock and gravel company. Fred has the sales expertise, while Barney runs the production side of the operation. Their overall profitability results from their joint efforts. If Fred were to die prematurely, Barney would have to either hire a new employee or promote someone to fill Fred's position. A new hire would be unlikely to duplicate Fred's results.
>
> At the same time, Fred's widow Wilma would want to continue to take the same money out of the business that they received before Fred's death. In fact, if Widow Wilma is raising a young family or has children in college, she may have to force a sale of the business at a distressed price just to meet her needs.
>
> Maybe Fred's daughter Pebbles feels like she was born to run the company and has her own ideas about how things should be run. Perhaps Widow Wilma wants to see their less popular son step into his father's role. It wouldn't matter that little Fredo is incompetent. There are so many problems that can arise. Needless to say, it may be impossible for Barney to continue a profitable business under such circumstances.

Unless you want to have to sell your business to pay your late partner's family or take on the spouse or child of your late partner as your new partner, you must plan. Only by planning can you and your partners answer these questions in a way that satisfies all parties, while enabling the business to be maintained. As mentioned earlier, the best tool for solving the dilemmas that arise from these questions is the buy-sell agreement, in its various forms.

The Buy-Sell Agreement

A buy-sell agreement is an agreement that all owners sign that stipulates how the business will be valued at the time of one partner's death or disability and how the purchase of the deceased partner's shares will be paid. There are various ways to structure buy-sell agreements, depending on the goals and circumstances of the owners, and the business itself. In all arrangements, there are some basics regarding buy-sell agreements that apply to any type of business. The benefits stakeholders can gain from a buy-sell agreement are universal.

Practically speaking, buy-sell agreements can be used for corporations, partnerships, limited partnerships, limited liability companies (LLCs) and other business structures as well. To simplify the text, we will use the words *business owner* generically, to mean any type of business owner, including, a shareholder in a corporation, partners in a partnership, and members in a LLC. In the list below, we discuss the benefits of a buy-sell agreement for the business and remaining owners, each owner, and the family.

Benefits to the business and remaining owners: First, a properly planned buy-sell agreement will provide for the orderly continuation of the ownership and control of the business in the event of death, disability, divorce, or bankruptcy of any owner, or the desire of any owner to retire. Second, the buy-sell agreement will prevent unwanted outsiders from becoming owners and eliminate the need for difficult negotiations with surviving spouses and children. By funding the agreement with life insurance and disability insurance policies, you provide liquidity for the business to purchase the outstanding ownership interests of the disabled or deceased partner.

Benefits to family members: The funded buy-sell agreement can assure the family or estate a liquid asset rather than an illiquid minority interest in a privately held business – which would be difficult to sell. The agreement itself may provide a valuation of the business interest, which can be used for estate tax filing purposes. This may save the survivors the additional headache and expense of securing another valuation and fighting the Internal Revenue Service on that value.

If one owner becomes disabled, the buy-sell contract guarantees that the disabled owner's family does not have to become involved in the business in order to protect the family's interest. This creates peace of mind as the disabled owner knows that he has retrieved his investment in the business and does not have to continue to worry about its future.

The Buy-Sell Agreement plus Disability Policies

Savvy business owners have signed buy-sell agreements, and they fund them with life insurance policies and lump sum disability policies on each of the partners. This ensures that any unforeseen misfortune doesn't destroy the business and hurt all of their families. Without the proper disability policies as part of a buy-sell agreement, a business will be severely disrupted and may fail.

Funding the Agreement

Because the buy-sell agreement contemplates a buy-sell transaction at the time of an owner's death or disability, insurance policies are generally recommended to fund the transaction. There are many reasons for this, including the following:

- Insurance policies pay a predetermined amount, with proceeds available at exactly the time when they are needed as a funding source (no liquidity concerns).
- Proceeds will be available regardless of the financial state of the business at that point (as long as premiums have been paid).
- The business leverages the cost of premiums to create the proceeds, thus, it costs the business less to buy insurance than it would cost to save money in a special buyout fund.
- The economic risks of early death or premature disability of any owner are shifted to the insurer.
- Insurance proceeds are paid to the owner or owner's family income-tax free.

A lump-sum cash payment through a disability insurance policy is ideal as it eliminates the need for personal guarantees from remaining owners, mortgages or security interests in real estate, a bank standby letter of credit, or even collaterally assigned life insurance policies.

The Need for a Coordinated Team

Creating a buy-sell arrangement that fits a particular business requires expertise and experience. Expertise in areas of corporate and business law, tax law, insurance products, and the valuation of businesses are all *absolute* requirements. It is just as important to have experience dealing with different owners, and the ability to negotiate and draft an agreement that meets the needs of all parties involved.

A coordinated buy-sell team would involve the following:

- An attorney who has experience creating buy-sell types of arrangements;
- A life and disability insurance professional who has worked on similar issues before; and,
- A business appraisal firm whose expertise may be needed on an ongoing basis for annual business valuations.

Charting a Better Path

As with any legal or insurance planning, the early bird is richly rewarded. Nowhere in business planning is this truer, than in buy-sell agreements. The reason for this is not so much economic, as it is political. If planning is carried out before an owner is close to disability, divorce, retirement, or death, all owners are in similar positions relative to one another. That makes the negotiation of a standard deal for all owners a much easier and smooth process. Planning early for a buy-sell agreement will benefit you, your family, your business partners, and your business. In order to avoid financial disaster, consider this agreement an essential part of your financial planning.

Buy-sell agreements don't just protect against death. They also protect against disability, which was discussed two chapters ago. Disability does not just affect business. A disability can devastate a family. Speaking of devastation, the next chapter will discuss perhaps the most traumatic event for any family – and only half of the families in America will deal with it. Continue to the next chapter to see how to protect your family wealth, your children, and your grandchildren from divorce.

Chapter 16
You Can't Cut a Giraffe in Half

"100% of Divorces Start with Marriage"

—Anonymous

"My husband and I have never considered divorce.
Murder sometimes, but never divorce."

—Dr. Joyce Brothers

Of all the risks to the affluent, the most common threat to financial security may be divorce. According to the U.S. Centers for Disease Control, 41 percent of marriages ended in divorce or annulment (http://www.cdc.gov/nchs/nvss/marriage_divorce_tables.htm).

The divorce rate increases substantially with second and third marriages. Besides being common, divorce is also an emotionally devastating experience and can be financially disastrous as well.

Divorce protection is not about hiding assets from a future ex-spouse. Nor is it about cheating or lying to keep your wealth. Rather, it concerns resolving issues of property ownership and distribution *before* things go sour. Spouses can spare themselves considerable money, time, and emotional distress in the long run by deciding in advance, who would get what, in the event of a divorce. This type of asset-protection planning inevitably benefits all parties, except the divorce lawyers, of course.

Divorce planning is also about shielding family assets from the potential divorces of children and grandchildren. Given the statistics enumerated above, it is almost a certainty that either your child or grandchild will get divorced. For purposes of intergenerational financial planning, this is a crucial topic, unless you want to give half of your inheritance to the ex-spouses of your heirs. This is something the wealthiest families have successfully navigated for decades. They don't have a secret for avoiding divorce. They have a secret for avoiding the financial losses that can be associated with divorce. This chapter will discuss why divorce can be so financially devastating, the pros and cons of prenuptial agreements, irrevocable trusts, and ways to protect your children from the financial effects of divorce *without* requiring them to sign prenuptial agreements.

Why Divorce Can Be a Financial Nightmare

Most Americans do not have to read newspapers to see how financially devastating a divorce can be. While high-profile divorces involving tens of millions of dollars dramatically illustrate the point, most of us need only look to family or friends to see how a divorce can create financial upheaval. One common attitude toward divorce is illustrated by a scene in the movie, *First Wives Club*. In the film, Ivana Trump explains her theory of divorce to three ex-wives, played by Goldie Hawn, Diane Keaton, and Bette Midler. "Don't get even," she says, "get everything!"

Combine this fight-for-everything attitude with the terrible odds of getting a divorce, and you have a very serious threat to financial security. In fact, a divorce threatens not only former spouses, but also their families and possibly their business partners. To truly understand how a divorce affects the finances of the participants, you must understand how property is divided when the marriage is dissolved.

Community Property States

Nine states have community property laws: Arizona, California, Idaho, Louisiana, Nevada, New Mexico, Texas, Washington, and Wisconsin. Community property law stipulates that if there is no valid pre- or post-marital agreement, the court will equally divide between the ex-spouses any property acquired during the marriage other than inheritances or gifts given directly to one spouse or the other. Even the appreciation of one spouse's separate property can be divided if the other spouse expended effort on that property during the marriage, and the property actually appreciated concurrent or subsequent to the effort expended. Based on these facts, it is obvious that how the asset is titled is not the controlling factor. Instead, when the asset was acquired and how it was treated are far more important factors in determining how the asset will be treated by the courts.

Equitable Distribution States

Non-community property states are called *equitable distribution states,* because courts in these states have total discretion to divide the property equitably and fairly. The court will normally consider a number of factors in deciding what is equitable, including the duration of the marriage, the age and conduct of the parties, and the current earnings and future earning potential of each former spouse. The danger of equitable divorces is that courts often distribute both non-marital assets (those acquired before the marriage) as well as marital assets (those acquired during marriage), equally between the divorcees. In this way, courts often split up property in ways that the ex-spouses never wanted or anticipated.

Examples of "Disaster Divorces"

We've included the following examples of divorces involving affluent couples in order to help you consider whether you and your family are adequately prepared for divorce.

Example 1. A couple marries. This is the second marriage for each and they both have adult children from their first marriages. Without any pre- or post-marital agreement, they title many of the wife's previously separate income-producing properties (such as her rental apartment units) into the name of the new husband in order to reduce their income tax burden. Within two years of the marriage, they divorce. The husband gets half the rental units (in addition to alimony and other property) even though both spouses understood that the wife intended them to go to her children. The court simply ignored their understanding, giving half of the couple's property to each spouse.

Example 2. A couple marries, each for the first time. Over the next 20 years, the husband acquires more ownership in his family's bakery business. His father, the founder, gradually transfers shares to him. At 42, he is the majority owner. He and his wife then undergo a bitter divorce, and the ex-wife is granted half the husband's bakery business as community property. She then forces high dividends and a sale of the company to a competitor.

Example 3. An internal medicine resident gets married. She and her husband discuss the cost of her medical education and agree that she should not have to compensate him for his greater financial contribution in the early years of their marriage. However, they file for divorce eight years later. The husband considers the wife's professional degree as marital property, so he claims a share in her earning potential. The court agrees, even though the couple verbally agreed to the contrary.

Can a Pre-nuptial Protect You?

A premarital agreement, or *prenuptial agreement,* premarital contract, or *ante-nuptial agreement,* is the foundation of any protection against a divorce. The premarital agreement is a written contract between the spouses. It specifies the division of property and income upon divorce, including disposition of specific personal property, such as family heirlooms. It also states the responsibilities of each party with regard to their children after divorce. Finally, these agreements lay out the respective responsibilities of each partner during marriage, such as the financial support each spouse can expect, and the religious education the children will receive.

Requirements for a Premarital Agreement

Each state differs slightly on what is required for an enforceable premarital agreement. The following are common requirements:

1. The agreement must be in writing and signed by both parties.
2. There must be a fair, accurate, and reasonable disclosure of each party's financial condition.
3. Each party must be advised by a separate attorney.
4. The agreement must not be unconscionable. Courts will not enforce a one-sided agreement.
5. The couple must follow the agreement during the marriage.
6. The person suggesting the premarital agreement must be willing to walk away from the marriage.

I have not seen the discussion of a prenuptial agreement go well with any clients or with their children – before the wedding day. As prudent as the idea is, it's a very difficult sale. This is why the next couple of solutions are easier and more effective.

Irrevocable Spendthrift Trusts: Ideal Tools to Keep Assets in the Family

As you will see in the **giraffeMONEY** ***Estate Planning Guide***, irrevocable trusts are very effective asset protection tools because neither the grantor, nor the beneficiaries, own the assets. The assets are legally owned by the trust. Creditors of beneficiaries, including ex-spouses, cannot invade the trust for its assets if they have not been distributed from the trust.

Nonetheless, using an irrevocable trust should not be considered lightly. Giving away assets forever with no strings attached can prove to be a serious consequence when protecting against divorce, lawsuit, or other threat. There are certain circumstances where this strategy makes sense, such as in circumstances where you would have inevitably given away the assets to certain beneficiaries anyway. For example, the trust might be used for assets that 1) you will leave to your children or grandchildren when you die; and 2) you do not need those assets for your financial security. For a more detailed example, consider the Irving's case study. Home

Protect Your Children from Divorce

When your children or grandchildren come to you, giddy with exciting news about their recent engagement, the last thing they want to hear you ask is, "Are you going to sign a prenuptial agreement?" In fact, if you weren't paying for the wedding, you might lose your invitation for asking such a question.

As you learned earlier, the secret to protecting assets from divorce is keeping the assets as separate property and not commingling them with community or marital property. You can't count on your children to do this, so you can do it for them, without requiring the consent of your child or the future (or existing) spouse.

By leaving assets to your children's irrevocable trusts, with appropriate spendthrift provisions, rather than to them personally, you can achieve this goal. Of course, if the children take money out of the trust and use it to buy a home or other property, that property will be subject to the rules of their state.

To illustrate this point, let's look at the example of Rob and Janelle, college sweethearts who got married right after graduation. Within a few years, their romance turned sour and Rob could no longer handle the physical and emotional abuse. However, during their three-year marriage, Janelle received a sizeable inheritance from her grandparents, and used it to pay off the couple's home. When they filed for divorce, Rob's attorney successfully argued that the time and labor he invested in the house, and the fact that he lived in it except when Janelle occasionally kicked him out, made half of the equity in the home ($100,000), Rob's fair share. Though Rob and his friends will argue the $100,000 was a small consolation for what he had endured, Janelle's grandparents certainly didn't intend for Rob to receive their inheritance.

What could Janelle have done differently to ensure that she protected her assets? Her grandparents could have left her the inheritance through an irrevocable trust that allowed her to withdraw limited amounts of money each year. In that case, she would have used the interest from the inheritance to pay the mortgage down each month. If she did so, the corpus of the inheritance would have remained separate property and would not have included in the divorce settlement. In the three short years of their marriage, they would have had little equity in their home and Rob would have left the marriage with the property that he brought into it, and his wounded pride—but none of Janelle's grandparents' life savings.

In a nutshell, a little proactive financial planning can go a long way to making sure that a divorce doesn't completely disrupt a family's financial situation.

Charting a Better Path

It is easy to understand why so few people are wealthy. It is next to impossible to become successful, and it can be lost to personal and professional lawsuits, disability, and divorce. Luckily, you have learned many ways to protect wealth from those threats. If you want to dive deeper into the many valuable estate planning tools that exist for moderately successful to super affluent families, please access the **giraffeMONEY** ***Estate Planning Guide*** at www.GiraffeUniversity.com/resources today.

Though each of the threats we saw along this path has the potential to devastate a family or a business, people roll the dice without protection – and many never have a problem. On the next path, you will encounter a threat that impacts every person and every business each and every year. If you do not focus on this, you will throw away unnecessary profit every year. Continue to the 4th Path to learn how to reduce the endless tolls on a giraffe's path to affluence.

4th PATH
Don't Waste Energy Playing with Zebra

"There is no need to use force. Instead, create a path of least resistance, and gravity will do the rest."

—Michael Dunlap

If a giraffe isn't careful, it may look at the zebra all around and get jealous. Most days, zebra don't have much to worry about. They follow the herd and eat the grass around them. If danger approaches, a member of the herd will let the rest know all about it. In their seemingly carefree existence, you will see the zebra play and run around. The young ones run and jump and try to get the other foals to play with them. The adults are constantly comparing themselves to other zebra – to see who can run faster or further. A translation of their barks and yips would probably be, "Bet you can't catch me" or "You're it. No, I tagged *you* last."

Giraffes keep their perspective and focus on the bigger picture. They don't want to waste unnecessary energy they might need for a long walk for food or water, to evade or fight against a hungry pride of lions.

In the last section, you saw the importance of avoiding devastating mistakes that could kill your business or deplete your assets. Here, you will learn how to avoid a death by a thousand cuts through taxes. Income tax, capital gains tax, and estate tax chip away at everything you have. In total, taxes will cost you more over your lifetime than any house, lawsuit, or equipment.

Using my math, finance and actuarial background, I have been hired by hundreds of very successful businesses owners and even a few billionaire families to help them legally reduce their tax burden by millions of dollars. Though the topic may be the most boring and complicated in this book, I assure you it is the single greatest planning focus of my company's most affluent clients.

As you strive to *manage* taxes, you must first *understand* taxes. These lessons are both the foundation for your new giraffe philosophy and the building blocks for powerful techniques you should consider. By the time you get to the end of this path, you will see how to legally minimize taxes for your family, learn when to sacrifice smaller tax payments today to create more value in your company, and know how to eliminate over $10 million in future gift or estate taxes with one simple planning technique.

Note: There may be references to different techniques, strategies and tools that are unfamiliar to you. More detailed tax information is available to you in the **giraffeMONEY** ***Tax Planning Guide*** at www.GiraffeUniversity.com/resources as well. Feel free to download it when you are ready to prioritize your tax planning.

Chapter 17
Uncle Sam Hunts Giraffes (Like You)

"The hardest thing to understand in the world is the income tax."
—Albert Einstein

You can't expect to successfully overcome any challenge until you fully understand the challenge itself. In this chapter, we will explain how great an effect taxes can have on your finances. We will also share techniques wealthy families have used for decades to successfully reduce unnecessary taxes.

As a geeky mathematician, I have always enjoyed solving problems. Every year since 1980, when my mom bought my first Rubik's Cube, she has sent me a different puzzle to solve. As a CERTIFIED FINANCIAL PLANNER™ Professional, I have successfully helped hundreds of entrepreneurs restructure their businesses to reduce unnecessary costs and to build additional value. I have had the pleasure of working with three billionaire families, who wanted to protect significant wealth. They didn't just want to protect the money from taxes, they also wanted to protect the children and grandchildren from the money!

I can appreciate the difficulty in navigating both the enormity of the Internal Revenue Code and the psychological complications money has for people. For that reason, I am going to follow the example of an idol of mine, John Wooden – the legendary college basketball coach from UCLA. It wasn't until I became friends with one of his favorite players, Jamaal Wilkes, that I had an opportunity to meet Coach Wooden. After meeting "The Wizard of Westwood," I started investigating his amazing teachings in basketball and in life. Wooden started every new season's first practice, with the best players in the country, by showing the players how to properly tie their shoes. It's much easier to trip when we aren't sure of our footing.

If it's good enough for Coach Wooden to start with basics, who am I to argue with such greatness? I promise this review is necessary for us to build a foundation for the more advanced strategies in the book.

Let's get started by examining where and how tax revenue is generated by looking at four types of taxes:

1. Taxes on money you earn;
2. Taxes on investments you make;
3. Taxes on assets you leave to your heirs; and
4. A hidden 70 percent tax few people know exists.

A Treasured Gift from Jamaal Wilkes

Income Taxes

Every citizen pays income taxes on salaries and other income. Do you know exactly how income taxes are computed? Most people believe that they move from income tax bracket to income tax bracket—increasing the percentage they pay on each dollar earned as advance. The truth is that every individual (filing single or separately) pays the same tax rate on the first $9,875 of income and every married couple filing jointly pays the same tax rate on the first $19,750 earned in 2020. As a taxpayer's income crosses a threshold into the next tax bracket, only the dollars earned within that bracket are taxed at the higher rate. Tables below illustrate how income tax is determined for single people and for married couples that filed jointly in 2020.

Single or Married filing Separately	
Marginal Tax Rate	**Income**
10%	$0 – $9,875
12%	$9,876 – $40,125
22%	$40,126 – $85,525
24%	$85,526 – $163,300
32%	$163,301 – $207,350
35%	$207,351 – $518,400
37%	$518,401 and higher

Married filing jointly and surviving spouses.	
Marginal Tax Rate	**Income**
10%	$0 – $19,750
12%	$19,751 – $80,250
22%	$80,250 – $171,051
24%	$171,051 – $326,600
32%	$326,600 – $414,700
35%	$414,701 – $622.050
37%	$622,051 and higher

Poorly Camouflaged *Additional* Income Taxes

Every citizen pays both Social Security and Medicare tax. In 2020, the combined rate for Social Security and Medicare is 7.65 percent. This amount is deducted from the employee's paycheck and the employer pays a matching rate. The Social Security portion (OASDI) is 6.2 percent and the Medicare portion is 1.45 percent. Social security applies on the first $137,7000 of income. Medicare applies on all earnings, with no limit.

Status	Rate
Employee	7.65%
Self-Employed	15.30%

As of January 2013, individuals with income over $200,000 or couples with income over $250,000 pay an additional 0.9 percent in Medicare Tax. The rates shown above do not reflect the extra 0.9 percent tax.

Taxes on Investments

Once you earn money and pay income taxes, you aren't done with tax payments. This is only the tip of the tax iceberg. You may spend the money you earn (after taxes) on small items and pay sales tax, or you may buy real estate and pay annual property taxes. Another possibility is that you save the money and invest it. Common investment choices of average Americans include savings accounts, certificates of deposit (CDs), money market funds, stocks, bonds, mutual funds, cash-value insurance policies, and real estate. Further information will be found along the 5th Path and more detailed reports are also available at www.GiraffeUniversity.com/resources.

Most investments are generally classified as either income or growth vehicles. In some cases, an investment may fit both classifications. Income investments are those that offer some type of regular return (income) to the investor. Your bank accounts, CDs, and money market funds give you an interest payment each year. If you own traditional bonds, you receive a coupon every six or 12 months. If you own rental real estate, you may collect rental income. All of these interest payments, bond coupon payments, and rent checks are added to your income for the purpose of calculating taxable income as discussed above. If you are in a 32 percent marginal income tax bracket, then you will have to pay tax of 32 percent on those payments. If you are in a 35 percent marginal tax bracket, then you will pay 35 percent of the investment gain in taxes on that investment income. Of course, if you are not in an income-tax-free state (most are not), you could pay up to 10 percent in additional state income tax as well.

Not all investors require immediate income from investments. Because the affluent don't need current income from investments, they can afford to invest in more risky investments while looking for greater long-term appreciation. The affluent are looking for growth vehicles such as stocks (usually small cap or technology types), hedge funds, certain types of mutual funds, individually managed accounts, and life insurance contracts that may have any of these vehicles as underlying investments.

Beware the Impact of Taxes of Mutual Funds

"Over the past 20 years, the average investor in a taxable stock mutual fund gave up the equivalent of 17 to 44 percent of their returns to taxes."*

**CNN/Money.com 4/17/07 quoting Lipper*

When you invest with a particular company, your money is used to help grow that firm. As the value of the company increases, the value of your shares in the company also increases. You may or may not receive a regular check (stock dividend) from the company. The value of the company will vary from day to day and you have the right to sell your shares of the company at any time. When you do sell, and you realize a profit on your investment, you arc responsible for taxes on your capital gains. For tax purposes, capital gains can be categorized as long-term or short-term. Short-term is defined as realized (sold) appreciation of an asset that you owned for less than one year. If you have a short-term gain, it is treated exactly the same way (for tax purposes) as the interest, coupons, and rental income described above. Of course, if their combined earned income and investment income reach $414,701, each additional dollar will be taxed at 35 percent.

If you hold an asset for more than one year, the government gives you a benefit. You can pay long-term capital gains tax rates on your realized appreciation. Currently, there are capital tax rates of 0,15, and 20 percent based on your taxable income (plus applicable state taxes).

Filing Status	0% rate applies when taxable income is	15% rate applies when taxable income is	20% rate applies when taxable income is
Single	Less than $40,000	$40,000 to $441,450	More than $441,450
Married Filing Jointly	Less than $80,000	$80,000 to $496,600	More than $496,600
Head of Household	Less than $53,600	$53,600 to $469,050	More than $469,050
Married Filing Separately	Less than $40,000	$40,000 to $248,300	More than $248,300

Source: IRS

This benefit provides an incentive to investors to keep their funds in one place. This stability is much better for the overall economy than is the constant buying and selling, which could significantly disrupt business. Note: for high income earners, there is also a 3.8 percent Medicare tax that could bring this long-term capital gains tax rate up to 23.8 percent - plus applicable state taxes.

Taxes will take inches off your neck and years off your life

You may think that a couple percentage points of taxes on your investments may not be much. In any given year, you would be right. But, over your lifetime, you might be surprised. To explain how a small differential each year can decimate your account, let's explore the Law of 72.

> The Law of 72 states that 72 divided by the annual after-tax rate of return of an investment will give you the number of years it takes an investment to double in value.
>
> At 9 percent, an investment doubles ever 8 years.
> At 6 percent an investment doubles every 12 years.
> At 3 percent, an investment doubles ever 24 years.

Under the Law of 72, an investment that returns 9 percent per year doubles in value every eight years. In 24 years, a $100,000 investment that grew by 9 percent per year would be worth $800,000. What would happen if this investor paid less attention to taxes? Would it make that much of a difference? Let's see.

A $100,000 investment with a 6 percent return would take 12 years to double in value (because 33 percent of the 9 percent pretax gain was eroded by taxes). At the end of 24 years, this investment would be worth $400,000. If your investments lose 33 percent of the return each year to taxes, you could end up with 50 percent less in your investment account at the end of 24 years.

How many years would you have to keep busting your ass working to make up for that $400,000 of squandered return? Those are the years you could lose by ignoring the long-term impact of taxes. The possibility of doubling your net return should be enough for you to pay attention to taxes for each of your investments.

Estate Taxes

When you die, Uncle Sam has an estate tax for those worth more than the estate tax exemption. Immediately before the multi-trillion-dollar bailouts from the corona virus pandemic, the exemption amount was $11.58 million per person. In recent years, the amount you legally pass on to future generations was $1 million per person. Your estate may include the combined value of your home, retirement plans, real estate, brokerage accounts, and insurance policies. While the federal estate tax rates might be between 40 percent (2020) and 55 percent (recent past), some states have their own state inheritance taxes that do not necessarily have the same exemption amount as the federal estate tax. This means that combined tax rates will vary significantly from state to state. For estimation purposes and to make the calculations easier, we will assume the estate tax rate to be about 50 percent throughout the book. That means that half of what you think you will leave your children could go to taxes. For a complete description of the estate tax, how it works, why the supposed repeal is a fairy tale, and how to avoid the unnecessary costs associated with it, please read the **giraffeMONEY** ***Guide to Estate Planning*** available at www.GiraffeUniversity.com/resources.

The Dreaded 70 Percent Tax

Lastly, there is a combination of taxes that severely threatens those of you who hope to be worth more than the exemption amount and who might die with a retirement plan, an individual retirement account (IRA), annuity, or any income from royalties, commissions, or unpaid salaries. If you would like to leave any of those assets to your children, there is something called income in respect of a decedent (IRD). This tax is a double tax and it devastates retirement plan balances. It will be discussed in greater detail along this path when you learn about the pros and cons of retirement plans. Just know that there are hidden threats in this tax code that can trap unknowing travelers.

Charting a Better Path

It may seem crazy that there are so many ways that you can lose your wealth to taxes. Our tax laws are among the most complex systems of rules ever created. We will never master them all, but we can hope to find a few ways to help manage the costs of complying with the system. We are hopeful that you understand how much money is at stake and will pay close attention as you journey down this path. Reducing taxes may prove to be the most essential secret of the affluent you will ever master. However, just when you think you have it all figured out – the laws change. Continue to the next chapter to see what might be just around the corner.

Chapter 18
Hunting Season is about to Get Longer

"The perils of duck hunting are great - especially for the duck."
—Walter Cronkite

When a hunter shoots its target with anything other than a fatal shot, the animal will certainly be startled. Its survival instinct will kick in and it will run off at great speed – despite the bleeding and the pain. What happens next depends on the animal. Some animals will be skittish of humans forever and will remain ever vigilant. Over time, others may develop a false sense of security – and end up a trophy on the wall or steaks in a deep freezer.

If you have experienced having a well above-average income year, you remember the startling feeling and the bleeding that went along with that big tax bill. Many high earners I know choose to vote with their checkbooks, hoping that politicians will relieve them of some of their tax burdens. I'm not judging them (or, maybe a little), but I do notice a similar behavior to the hunted animal above. Some giraffe earners and builders become extremely vigilant of taxes and never let their guard down. Others become complacent after seeing the first tax law change to their advantage. Their fatal (financial) mistake? They don't act on all of the tax law changes when they are in their favor and then one day – BOOM! They get shot. A new president or the new balance of power in Congress, or some unexpected national disaster, and taxes go up quickly.

Taxpayers need to think of themselves as animals and understand that tax laws are like hunting season. There are really good times, and there are some very risky times. You must take advantage of the laws when they are in your favor – because they could change quickly and an amazing opportunity to permanently remove millions of dollars of taxes could be gone forever.

Where Are We in the Income Tax Season?

If you look at the history of the highest marginal tax rates in the table below, you can see that these rates have moved considerably over the last century.

Federal Income Taxes	
Year	**Highest Marginal Rate**
1920	73.00%
1930	25.00%
1940	81.10%
1950	91.00%
1960	91.00%
1970	71.75%
1980	70.00%
1990	28.00%
2000	39.60%
2010	35.00%
2020	37.00%
Source: TheAtlantic.com accessed April 2, 2020	

Federal income tax rates are currently at a historical low and will likely rise, possibly significantly, in the future. Outside of the decade after the Great Depression, the highest marginal income tax rate was more than double what it is today for the better part of 60 years. Could the unpredictable coronavirus and its costly impact on the country lead to higher rates in the near future? Are you willing to bet your hard-earned money that rates will not increase?

What's the Best Season to Invest?

In 2020, our capital gains tax rates in the United States are near the lowest point they have been in our history. They are lower today than at any point in the last century.

Federal Capital Gains Taxes	
Year	**Top Rate**
1940	30.0%
1942-1967	25.0%
1970	32.3%
1977	39.9%
1980	28.0%
1990	28.0%
2000	20.0%
2010	15.0%
2013	20.0%
2020	20.0% to 23.8%

Note: For $250,000 earners, there is an additional 3.8 percent Medicare tax added to capital gains tax rates.

It's hard enough to earn money and pay income taxes, so savvy investors don't want to give away an unnecessary portion of their investment gains too. It's easy to see that capital gains tax rates are very low now and could become much higher in the relatively near future without surpassing the highest rates in history.

Is Uncle Sam's triple-dip enough? No, it isn't. After you pay your income taxes, sales taxes for your purchases, property taxes on real estate, and taxes on all of your investment gains, there is still more tax to be paid.

The Ever-Changing Landscape of Estate Taxes

In addition to the taxes above, there is also a tax on money you leave to the next generation. Each person is allowed to leave the "exemption" amount. The taxes on any amounts above the exemption are subject to a graduated estate tax. Over the last 23 years, these amounts have varied considerably.

Historical Gift Tax Exemption Amounts (Per Person)		
Year	**Estate Tax Exemption**	**Top Estate Tax Rate**
1997	$600,000	55%
1998	$625,000	55%
1999	$650,000	55%
2000	$675,000	55%
2001	$675,000	55%
2002	$1,000,000	50%
2003	$1,000,000	49%
2004	$1,500,000	48%
2005	$1,500,000	47%
2006	$2,000,000	46%
2007	$2,000,000	45%
2008	$2,000,000	45%
2009	$3,500,000	45%
2010	$5,000,000 or $0	35% or 0%
2011	$5,000,000	35%
2012	$5,120,000	35%
2013	$5,250,000	40%
2014	$5,340,000	40%
2015	$5,430,000	40%
2016	$5,450,000	40%
2017	$5,490,000	40%
2018	$11,180,000	40%
2019	$11,400,000	40%
2020	$11,580,000	40%
The Tax Cut And Jobs Act expires in 2025		
Source: IRS, FinancialSamurai.com		

As recently as 2001, the exemption amount was $675,000. That means a married couple could leave $1,350,000 tax free to their kids tax free. In 2020, the number exploded to $23,160,000. The highest estate tax rate in last 20 years has been 55 percent. It is at 40 percent now. A friend of mine, Chris Erblich, is a talented estate planning attorney at Husch Blackwell. His client list is filled with billionaires, deca-millionaires, and many famous people I can't share here. Suffice to say, he knows a lot of people with a great deal of money. He calls the past three years, the "golden age" of estate planning. Why are the advisors to millionaires and billionaires so happy with the recent situation?

1) Our exemptions are so much greater than ever before
2) Tax rates are low – relatively speaking
3) Interest rates are low – so we can lend money out of estates
4) We have tools today that we never had before

Chris's top piece of advice for anyone in 2020 is: "Do your estate planning NOW – before all these gifts we have are taken back!"

Beware the Second Shooter: Your State

In addition to all of the federal taxes, all but seven states have their additional income taxes. Though the state tax rates are much lower than the federal tax rates, their tax brackets tend to graduate more quickly In California, tax rates start at 1 percent, but escalate through six different rates to 9.3 percent for a single person earning $57,824 or a couple earning $115,648. There are four additional tax brackets as earners approach $1million of income. At this level they start paying 13.3 percent of their income to the California Franchise Tax Board.

Lowest and Highest Income Tax Rates By State

Alabama 2% - 5%	**Alaska** No Income Tax	**Arizona** 2.59% - 4.5%	**Arkansas** 2% - 6.6%	**California** 1% - 13.3%
Colorado 4.63%	**Connecticut** 3% - 6.99%	**Delaware** 2.2% - 6.6%	**District of Columbia** 4% - 8.95%	**Florida** No Income Tax
Georgia 1% - 5.75%	**Hawaii** 1.4% - 11%	**Idaho** 1.12% - 6.92%	**Illinois** 4.95%	**Indiana** 3.23%
Iowa 0.33% - 8.53%	**Kansas** 3.1% - 5.7%	**Kentucky** 5%	**Louisiana** 2% - 6%	**Maine** 5.8% - 7.15%
Maryland 2% - 5.75%	**Massachusetts** 5%	**Michigan** 4.25%	**Minnesota** 5.35% - 9.85%	**Mississippi** 3% - 5%
Missouri 1.5% - 5.4%	**Montana** 1% - 6.9%	**Nebraska** 2.46% - 6.84%	**Nevada** No Income Tax	**New Hampshire** 5%
New Jersey 1.4% - 10.75%	**New Mexico** 1.7% - 4.9%	**New York** 4% - 8.82%	**North Carolina** 5.25%	**North Dakota** 1.1% - 2.9%
Ohio 2.85% - 4.8%	**Oklahoma** 0.5% - 5%	**Oregon** 5% - 9.9%	**Pennsylvania** 3.07%	**Rhode Island** 3.75% - 5.99%
South Carolina 0% - 7%	**South Dakota** No Income Tax	**Tennessee** 1%	**Texas** No Income Tax	**Utah** 4.95%
Vermont 3.35% - 8.75%	**Virginia** 2% - 5.75%	**Washington** No Income Tax	**West Virginia** 3% - 6.5%	**Wisconsin** 4% - 7.65%
Wyoming No Income Tax				

source: tax-rates.org

Would You Die for Your State?

No, this is not a civil war reference. I am talking about the hidden cost of living and dying in a particular state. Prior to 2001, the federal estate tax rate was capped at 55 percent. The Federal Government kept 39 percent of the total tax and gave 16 percent to the various states. This was called a *sponge tax* because the states *soaked up* their portion of the total tax. Most states had no need to impose estate tax other than the amount they would receive from the federal estate tax return (Form 706). This scheme was repealed by the Economic Growth and Tax Relief Reconciliation Act of 2001 (EGTRRA). This Act is also known as "Bush Tax Cuts," as it was signed into law by President George W. Bush. The law became effective for individuals dying after 2004.

The estate tax reduction from 55 to 45 percent was seen as a savings to taxpayers, but what it really did was eliminate the states' piece of the estate tax as of 2004. The Federal Government actually keeps more of the taxes it collects than it did before the repeal – at the states' expense.

Unsurprisingly, the states were not happy to lose out on this tax revenue. To fight this tax loss, many states instituted their own taxes – either *state estate taxes* or *state inheritance taxes*. In the case of state death taxes, the rates may be lower than the federal tax rates but are not insignificant. Delaware, Hawaii, Illinois, Iowa, Kentucky, Minnesota, Maryland, Massachusetts, Nebraska, New Jersey, New York, Oregon, Rhode Island Vermont, and Washington have top rates of 15 to 20 percent.

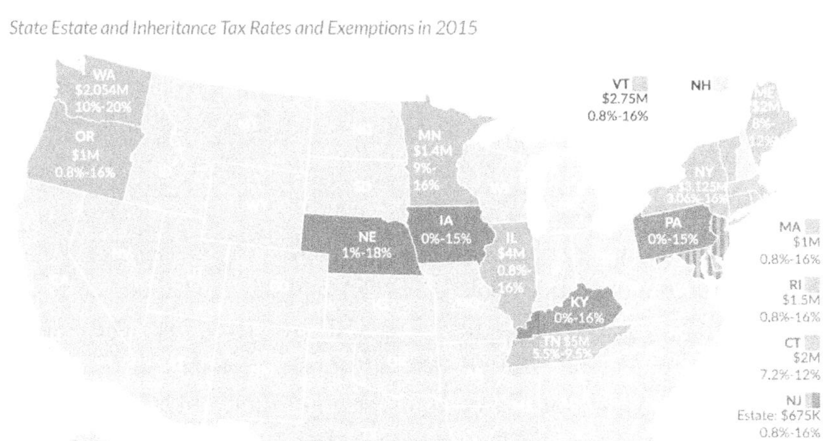

But wait, there's more!

In the case of state estate taxes, the exemption (or get out of taxes free card) are nothing like the Federal Unified Tax Credit of $11,580,000. Most states have exemptions of $1 to $2 million before applying their own estate taxes. So, even if you are not worth enough to owe federal estate tax, you could be lulled into a false sense of security and still get hit with a 20 percent state estate tax on millions of dollars.

In the case of state inheritance taxes, each charges a tax on *all* assets left as an inheritance within the state's jurisdiction. Unlike estate taxes, there is no exemption for state inheritance taxes. People in those states will pay taxes of up to 18 percent of their total assets if they do not plan accordingly.

As a result of the unintended consequences of the so-called "estate tax repeal" from 2001, wealthy families can actually pay combined federal and state taxes that are far more than they paid under the old system. Further, average families now have to pay state inheritance taxes starting at dollar one.

Charting a Better Path

The cumulative effect of taxes can be devastating to any significant earner. When I started writing this book, the main point of this chapter was to point out that tax rates are cyclical – they go up and down over time. The wealthiest families go out of their way to take advantage of favorable law changes immediately – so they don't lose out on the opportunity. In light of the recent stimulus package, there will be *trillions* of dollars of additional Federal Government expenditures. These are on top of an already imbalanced budget. Regardless of who wins the presidential and congressional elections in the fall of 2020, federal taxes will have to be raised to pay for this.

The Federal Government isn't alone in its dilemma; the states will have their own challenges. Look for increased state income taxes, property taxes, sales taxes and even state estate and inheritance taxes. There is no other way to pay for the expensive situation that was created in 2020. Do your planning now before the amazing benefits we have now are removed – and possibly never reinstated. If you want my team to take a look at your tax situation, feel free to contact me through www.chrisjarvis.me/contact.

Chapter 19
It's No Walk in the Park – Beware Retirement Plan Traps

"Youth is wasted on the young. Why do we retire when we don't have the energy to do anything with all that time off?"

—Ray Jarvis

We have just finished discussing taxes and how critical it is to reduce their impact. It makes sense to take advantage of as many deductions as legally possible. A basic philosophy in the tax code is to reward taxpayers with deductions when they invest in a vehicle that could reduce the burden to the government. That makes sense. Employers get deductions when they pay salaries. Those workers are not on welfare assistance. Employees and employers receive deductions for contributions for health insurance – reducing the government's obligation to support their health care. An extension of that benefit is the deduction for contributions to qualifying retirement plans.

If your employer offers to match your contributions, it's a good idea to put away a portion of your income into a sponsored plan. This will reduce your taxable income, force you to save for retirement, and will provide "free money" from your employer. These are all good things, so what's the catch?

Retirement Plans are Not "Giraffe-Sized"

There are many types of tax-deductible retirement vehicles. They fall into one of two categories: *defined contribution plans* or *defined benefit plans.* Defined contribution plans restrict the amount you can *contribute* to the plans on an annual basis. These include all forms of individual retirement accounts (IRAs), profit sharing plans, money purchase plans, 401(k) plans, and others. Defined benefit plans restrict how much money you can accumulate in the plan for your *benefit.* We will revisit those shortly.

The first mathematical problem with these plans is they were created at a time when people worked until 60 or 65, and seldom lived in their 80s or beyond. In 1950, life expectancy in the United States was 68 years. In 2020, our population's life expectancy is 79. While that is only 11 years, it is an enormous increase in the number of years people are expected to live during retirement. Though the contribution limits have gone up over time, they have not kept pace with the increase in life expectancy.

The second problem is that plans were designed to meet the needs of average to moderately successful people. An IRA only allows you to contribute $19,500 per year. Even if you could max out the plan, how much could you possibly accumulate over 30-40 years of working? Certainly not enough to maintain your quality of life for 20-30 years in retirement.

The percentage of income calculations of certain plans cap out at $285,000 of gross income. If you earn (or hope to earn more) more than $285,000 per year, you will need to find alternative savings vehicles to help you accumulate enough to retire.

The Silver Special: Over 50 Catch-Up Options

Imagine the fear of being 50 years old, or older, and realizing that you don't have enough money saved for retirement. How could this happen? Maybe you never took retirement seriously. Perhaps you failed to save enough. Half of the country gets divorced – you could have been on track and then lost half of your retirement plan. It's even possible that some national or global emergency caused the stock market to tank. In that instance, many people access funds in their plans to pay bills. Others are set back years, if not decades, in accumulating retirement savings.

With the IRA mentioned above, the IRS allows people over 50 to contribute an additional $6,500 per year – bringing the maximum tax-deductible contribution up to $26,000 per year. That's a significant increase (on a percentage basis), but $6,500 per year isn't going to make up for starting late, getting divorced, or suffering a stock market meltdown.

The defined benefit ("DB") plan may be a solid option for silver giraffes who own their own businesses (or who have a lot of influence over their employers who do). DB plans are very different from defined contribution ("DC") plans that base annual contributions on a percentage of income. The DB plans works backwards. Actuaries start by calculating how much the participant will require in a plan on the day of retirement to secure income for the remainder of his life.

Procrastinators Actually Win

Why is the DB formula beneficial? If you failed to contribute to your 401(k) or IRA for 30 years, then only had 10 years to fund your DB plan, you might be able to contribute $100,000 to $200,000 per year – and deduct all of those contributions from your taxable income. Look at this example:

> **Clayton Paddled Out Late; Caught A Bigger Wave**
> After pursuing a professional surfing career for decades, Clayton went to business school, received his MBA, and began a lucrative consulting career. After working for a big five firm for two to three years, he started his own business. At this point, he was 50 years old and had no retirement savings. We helped him create a DB plan for his corporation and our calculations showed that, based on his age of 50 and his salary of $175,000, he would be able to put away $69,000 per year (on a tax-deductible basis). This saved Clayton over $30,000 in income taxes and helped him begin recouping the time he lost in saving for his retirement. He also implemented other strategies that are described later in this section.

Are you a good candidate for a defined benefit plan?

Defined benefit plans are very attractive for individuals who:

- Are at least 50 years old
- Want to contribute more than defined contribution limits allow
- Have less in their retirement plan accounts than they should
- Don't' have too many highly-paid, or similar aged employees

There are many factors in determining the amount you can contribute to a DB plan and the requirements change each year. Most plan administrators will need a complete employee census that shows the names, dates of birth, sex, marital status, salary, years of service, and hours per week for every employee who has worked for the corporation for a given year to give you an accurate proposal. If you would like a retirement plan analysis and a proposal of options for you and your company, please contact me at info@chrisjarvis.me.

Ta Da! – Uncle Sam has a few tricks up his sleeve

A close friend of mine, Jim Munroe, is an accomplished illusionist who has performed all over the world. He once told me, there are only six tricks in magic:

1) Make something disappear
2) Make something reappear
3) Make something transform
4) Destroy something and restore it
5) Levitate something
6) A series of mindpowers

Uncle Sam is adept at a couple of these. We already have seen how Uncle Sam can make your money disappear. That's no big surprise. Let's see how his big trick may leave you debating which trick he performed on you.

What happens when you take advantage of the retirement planning laws and you properly fund your retirement plan? You receive a nice tax deduction every year. When the assets grow, you do not have to pay capital gains taxes. What a gift from your Uncle Sam. But wait! When you take money out of your plan, the taxes reappear AND they come back at ordinary income tax rates. That's right. You avoid income taxes and defer the lower capital gains taxes on the growth, but every dollar that comes out of your plan has been transformed to the higher tax rate. Ta da!!!!

To prove Magic Jim right again, the same holds true with another common retirement tool – annuities. Now most annuities are funded with after tax dollars (without any deduction for the contributions). However, taxes on the growth disappear. Until you take those gains out of the annuity. They also transform into ordinary income for tax purposes. Presto!

Big Finale: Income in Respect of Decedent

What happens when you save enough money in your retirement plans and annuities, and you don't spend it all? Perhaps you die earlier than expected, or you didn't need the retirement money because you had plenty of non-retirement dollars to take care of yourself. Most people would call you frugal or prudent. Uncle Sam may call you something different.

No tax discussion is complete without mentioning Income in Respect of a Decedent (IRD), which refers to the taxation of income earned by a deceased person who either didn't pay tax on the income before passing away or hadn't received the money before death. This income would have been taxable had the decedent lived long enough to receive it. Examples include unpaid salaries, bonuses and commissions, as well as qualified retirement plans (such as pensions and 401[k]s), roll-over IRAs, and variable annuity appreciation. Statistically, the qualified retirement plan and IRA balances are by far the most significant IRD assets.

One of the supposedly common-sense lessons repeated in the financial media is that you should contribute as much as you can to your retirement plans (pensions, profit-sharing plans, individual retirement accounts [IRAs], 401[k] plans, and so forth). The conventional wisdom is that because these plans offer an income-tax deduction and tax-deferred growth, they are a no-lose proposition.

This is another example of how conventional wisdom is detrimental for the giraffe. Retirement plans are a potentially dangerous tax trap for three reasons:

1. Likely, the participant will ultimately pay income taxes at the same or higher rates when taking distributions from the plan as he or she did while earning.
2. The client may not need most (or all) of the funds in retirement.
3. Perhaps most damaging, taxes will erode any funds left in these plans at death. Quite literally, these plans act as *traps,* capturing huge sums that are eaten up at tax rates of up to 70 percent.

Basics of Income in Respect of a Decedent

Income in respect of a decedent is income that would have been taxable to the decedent had the decedent lived long enough to receive it. Whomever receives these items of IRD must report them as gross income and pay any resulting income taxes in the year in which the items are received. Generally, that is the year of death however spouses are entitled to defer IRD until payments are withdrawn.

The IRD is taxable income that is assessed taxation in addition to any federal estate (death) taxes and state estate or inheritance taxes. Combined federal and state income tax rates (including those characterized as IRD) can be 45 percent or more in many states. Federal estate tax is currently capped at 40 percent -- but that doesn't include state inheritance taxes and any future increases to the federal estate tax. When you combine both taxes, the total tax on assets characterized as IRD assets can be more than 70 percent.

Case Study: Jim loses his retirement plan

Jim is an unmarried professor whose assets exceed the current estate-tax exemption. His IRA is fully taxable as it was funded entirely with tax-deductible contributions. (The same illustration is true for a married couple, but the estate tax wouldn't be due until the second spouse dies assuming that individual was the plan beneficiary due to the unlimited marital deduction.)

Assuming Jim's fully taxable IRA has a value of $1 million at his death, Jim's estate (or heirs) would first pay $460,000 in federal estate taxes and state inheritance taxes. His heirs would then pay another $251,212 in state and federal income taxes (45 percent of the remaining amount after giving a deduction for Federal estate taxes paid). Thus, only $283,780 is left out of the IRA for Jim's beneficiaries—less than 29 percent. More than 70 percent of the funds—built over a lifetime of working and paying income taxes—were taken by the IRD tax system.

The good news is that there are three (3) solutions to the dreaded IRD problem. If you, your spouse, or your parents have over $250,000 in retirement plan balances that won't be needed to pay for living expenses, and you desire to more tax-efficiently leave them for others to use, you will want to download the **giraffeMONEY** ***Estate Planning Guide*** at www.GiraffeUniversity.com/resources. If you would like my firm's assistance, or want an introduction to someone in your area who is familiar with circumstances like yours, please contact me at www.chrisjarvis.me/contact and someone will get back to you right away.

Charting a Better Path

Nobody wants to pay 70 percent tax on any assets. The tactic that successful investors use to supplement retirement income, is to maximize the use of tools and techniques that mirror many of the benefits of retirement plans. Because retirement plan contributions are limited, and the annual contribution amounts are based on the retirement needs of average Americans, the affluent need to utilize alternative saving and investment methods to meet their significantly higher, long-term retirement needs. A common strategy to enhance long-term retirement income, and reduce taxes on investment gains, is to invest in tax-favored financial instruments. When done correctly, this strategy can bear additional fruit in the form of increased value of your company. Because of this amazing benefit, we call this structure TrEE. It is covered in greater detail along the 5th Path.

Chapter 20
Where There's a "Will," There's a Pay(ment)

"If you want happiness for a year, inherit a fortune.
If you want happiness for a lifetime, help someone else."
—Confucius

In the complicated world of estate planning, small mistakes can be costly to both zebra and giraffes. A strategy that seems wise in the short term, can come back to bite you in the butt down the road. Here are three common mistakes I see with almost every client.

Mistake #1: Losing Money, Time, Privacy, & Control

One of the most prevalent mistakes in any estate plan is the unnecessary cost of probate. Probate is the process the state uses to process your estate. The purpose of probate is to make sure the rightful heirs receive their inheritance. If you don't have a will, only have a will, or have a living trust that does not own every single asset you have, then your estate will go through probate.

During probate, attorneys and courts rack up expenses that could amount to three to eight percent of the gross value of all of your assets (with no offset for liabilities like mortgages). If you own assets in multiple states (such as a vacation or rental home), your will must be probated again in each additional state where you own property. In addition to the expense of probate, your heirs may need to pay federal and state estate tax bills and your assets are tied up until probate is settled. God forbid you leave a business that needs to make a major change or have stocks you would like to sell. Probate delays could be catastrophic for your family.

Probate is a public process in all states. Anyone interested in your estate can find out who inherits under your will, how much he or she inherits, the beneficiaries' addresses, and more. While you may not be famous or worry about the newspapers exploiting this information, think of your surviving family members. They certainly will not appreciate the many financial advisors, or nefarious opportunists, calling them with hot tips on investments. These salespeople find beneficiaries by examining probate records.

In probate, the courts control the timing and final decisions on whether your will, and the wishes expressed in your will, are followed. Your family must abide by the court orders and pay for the process as well. This can be expensive and frustrating – especially when you had different plans for the inheritance than the state determined.

Mistake #2: Accidentally Disinheriting People

Joint ownership is the most popular form of ownership for average Americans' real-estate holdings and bank accounts. With joint property, when one owner dies, the property automatically passes to the surviving joint owner – completely bypassing the will and avoiding the expense of probate. This may appear to solve the problem with the first mistake above, but it can lead to much bigger problems.

In the eyes of the law, this automatic transfer takes effect the instant you die, before any will or living trust can dispose of your property. If you designated certain beneficiaries in a will or trust to receive your share of jointly held property, they will be disinherited, and the surviving joint owners will receive it. Consider these stories:

1. William has remarried and titled his home, vacation condo, and stock portfolio jointly with his second wife. When he dies, the home, condo, and stocks all go to William's new wife. His three children and eight grandchildren inherit virtually nothing, even though William had made ample provisions for them in his will.
2. Susan's will bequeaths her property to her son and daughter equally. Because her son lives nearby and helps her, Susan changed the title of her house, safe deposit box, and bank account to jointly own them with him. When she dies, Susan's son will get all of the money in the bank account and safe deposit box, as well as the house, regardless of the provisions of the will. Unless the son is extremely generous, the daughter will get close to nothing.
3. Cecilia, a single mother, is trying to build a college fund for her eight-year-old daughter, Debbie. Cecilia has invested her excess income into old multi-family homes, which she and her partner fix up and rent to tenants. Cecilia titles the investment properties

in joint ownership with her partner without realizing that if she dies before they resell the properties, her partner will get it all. He daughter will get nothing.

Many well-intentioned people get stuck in these predicaments because they do not know a better way, and their advisors are not doing a good job looking after their interests. Sometimes, owners may not even realize what type of ownership they have chosen. In other cases, people consciously decide to use joint ownership because they know it will avoid probate. Avoidance of probate is never a reason to use joint ownership.

Mistake #3: Surrendering $11 Million of Tax-free Transfers

In an attempt to simplify the estate planning process, most couples accidentally give away free exemptions that could save their heirs upwards of $5 million in unnecessary taxes at death. How? Let's look at the two fundamental elements of our estate-tax system:

- **Unified Tax Credit (UTC):** The UTC translates into a dollar amount that can be left by a decedent estate-tax free (commonly called the *estate-tax exemption*). This exemption was $600,000 in 1997, when I started working in this field 25 years ago. It grew to $1M in 2002, was $2M as recently as 2008, and is currently set at $11,580,000 for 2020. If a married couple utilizes their exemptions carefully, they could leave $23,160,000 tax free to heirs.

  I like to call the UTC a *get-out-of-estate-taxes-free* card, similar to the *get out of jail free* card in the board game Monopoly. Every one of us gets one of these cards to use either during our lives, or at the time of our deaths. However, the card is nontransferable and, if not used at death, is lost forever.
- **The Unlimited Marital Deduction (UMD):** The UMD rule means that a decedent can leave an unlimited amount to a surviving spouse without any estate tax—provided both spouses are U.S. citizens. Bill Gates could leave $60B to Melinda Gates at this death and there would be no estate tax.

  While this seems innocuous when the first spouse dies, the IRS has another trick up its sleeve that it pulls out later. When the surviving spouse dies, it's estate can only make use of one exemption. That means everything over the exemption amount will be subject to estate taxes—at rates above 40 percent. With the 2020 exemption amount at $11.58M, the federal estate taxes alone could be $4,632,000.

By owning assets jointly with your spouse, children, or business partner, you can cost your family up to 8 percent of your gross estate, waste nearly $5M of estate tax free transfers, lock up your assets at a time when your family needs them most, and possibly have your wishes for your inheritance disregarded by the state. These are horrible outcomes, but there is an easy fix.

Leverage: One Tool Solves All 3 Problems

The magic legal tool everyone worth more than $50,000 needs to implement, review, and update is the Living Trust. It is also referred to as a *loving trust, family trust, or A-B trust.* A living trust is a revocable trust, meaning you can change it at any time. During your lifetime, the assets transferred to the trust are managed and controlled by you, the trustee, just as if you owned them in your own name. When you die, these trust assets pass to whomever you designated in the trust, automatically, outside of the probate process. The living trust is the building block of estate planning as it offers your family relief from all of the problems in the previous chapter, and so many more.

Benefits of a Properly Funded Living Trust

- Avoids the unnecessary costs of probate
- Avoids unintentional disinheritances
- Keeps details of estate, and beneficiaries, private
- Saves your family up to $5,000,000 of taxes at death
- Ensures your wishes for inheritances are honored
- Prevents court control of assets if you become incapacitated
- Protects dependents with special needs
- Provides for guardians of children if you are incapacitated

The living trust is a simple tool for an estate planning attorney to create for you, but the nuances of what it can and should include are too detailed for this book. We will provide an overly simple overview here. If you want more detailed information about the living trust, how it works, how to use a pour-over will, and how to avoid the many pitfalls of trusts, you should download the **giraffeMONEY** ***Estate Planning Guide*** at www.GiraffeUniversity.com/resources.

How Does a Living Trust Work During Your Life?

Once you create a living trust, it is imperative that you transfer assets to the living trust. This is also known as *funding the trust.* If you create a trust and don't fund it with assets, it is completely useless.

When you transfer your assets to your living trust while you are alive, you maintain 100 percent control over these assets as though you still own them in your own name. There are no tax ramifications for transferring assets into your living trust. For your car, stocks, bonds, bank accounts, home, or any other asset, the process of transferring an asset to your living trust is the same. If the asset has a registration or deed, change the name on the document. If the asset is jewelry or artwork that has no official ownership record, use an assignment document to officially transfer ownership to your living trust.

These ownership changes will transfer the name of the registration or deed from John Doe to the "John Doe Revocable Living Trust" or "John Doe, Trustee of John Doe Revocable Living Trust." As sole trustee of the trust, you have the same power to buy, sell, mortgage, invest, and so on, as you did before. Because the trust is revocable, you can change beneficiaries or terms, remove or add assets, or even cancel your trust entirely.

Lego Giraffe: Living Trust Has Many Pieces

When you create your living trust, you can mix and match so many different elements, including:

- *Trustee. You may name yourself or someone else as trustee.* Most people name themselves during their lifetimes. At death, you could name an adult child, another relative, or close friend, or even a corporate trustee, such as a local bank or trust company. However, if you do not like the way the outside trustee is handling the trust, you have the power to remove him or her.

- *Timing. You decide when your beneficiaries receive their inheritances.* Another significant advantage of a living trust over a will is that you, rather than the courts, decide when and how your beneficiaries receive their inheritances. This can take as little time as weeks, be paid over years, or be contingent upon certain benchmarks.

How Does a Living Trust Work When You Die?

The living trust has no real purpose during your lifetime. When using an A-B living trust, the property is divided into two buckets, bucket A (or Trust A) and bucket B (or Trust B), at the death of the first spouse. Most people transfer assets that are the equivalent of the UTC amount into bucket B, which ultimately goes to the heirs. The balance of the property is then transferred to Trust A – using the unlimited marital exemption. In this way, there is no estate tax due and the exemption of the first spouse is salvaged.

It is true that the surviving spouse does not technically own Trust B, but he or she will have the ability to draw income and interest from the trust. More specifically, the surviving spouse may be able to live in the home; use the assets for health, education, maintenance and support; and typically use up to either five percent of the principal or $5,000 a year for any reason whatsoever.

After the death of the second spouse, the Trust B assets go directly to the heirs without any estate taxes. This is true even if the value of the assets has grown to equal more than the UTC amount. Trust A, which belonged to the surviving spouse, will also be distributed to the named beneficiaries. If the value of the Trust A assets exceeds the UTC amount, then that portion of the estate will be subject to estate taxes. After paying federal and state estate taxes, the assets will be transferred to the heirs.

Charting a Better Path

Estate tax laws are very complicated. When you add each of the fifty states' different rules for handling inheritances, you understand why so many taxpayers get confused. The biggest bang for your estate planning buck is to create, and fund, a living trust. For less than $5,000 of legal fees, a couple can eliminate costly probate and accidental disinheritances, keep their estate private, and avoid unnecessary estate taxes of up to $5 million.

This is some of the biggest leverage described in this book. If you already have an estate plan with a living trust, I highly recommend you pay someone to review it. It might cost you a thousand dollars, but you will get an outsider's opinion to make sure you haven't missed anything as federal and state laws have changed and your family assets have too.

Chapter 21
What Really Ticks a Giraffe Off?

"There are worse things in in life than death.
Have you ever spent an evening with an insurance salesman?"
—Woody Allen

Like attorneys, insurance agents have a bad reputation – which may be warranted. Having worked in the actuarial department of an insurance company, served as president of a reinsurance company, consultant to dozens of insurance companies and hundreds of insurance agents, and the owner of an insurance agency, I understand why people struggle with understanding life insurance.

There are many variables to consider. It is difficult to compare companies – they have different financial ratings and offer products with various bells and whistles. Even within the same company, there are multiple types of products (these different products are explained in greater detail in the **gira*ffe*MONEY** ***Insurance Guide***, available at www.GiraffeUniversity .com/resources. Once you choose a company and a product, the pricing isn't set until you go through health underwriting and are given a rating. People can waste a lot of money:

- Buying life insurance the wrong way;
- Owning life insurance the wrong way;
- Using life insurance the wrong way; and
- Cancelling life insurance the wrong way.

These mistakes could cost you, your family, or your business 20, 50 or 100 percent of your premiums. This chapter is designed to show you how to avoid those mistakes, so you get the most out of your life insurance.

Mistake #1: Overpaying for Life Insurance

There are hundreds of insurance companies and thousands of products to choose from in the life insurance arena. Insurance is heavily regulated – through each state's Department of Insurance ("DOI"). Every company must file its products, and its complicated classifications for pricing, with each state's DOI. Once filed and approved, those are the only products the company can offer in that state. Companies cannot customize products to individual consumers – and they are not allowed to provide discounts that are not part of their approved pricing algorithm.

Given these strict rules, you might think that there is nothing you can do to significantly lower your cost of insurance. If that were the case, we wouldn't be writing about it. Like many areas of business, giraffes look for places where they can use their elevated perspectives to find better paths. The underwriting function of life insurance is one of those places. Underwriting is important because it rates each potential insured's health – with each class paying a different amount for each $1,000 of death benefit (often referred to as "cost per thousand").

A big issue is that you don't know exactly how much you are going to pay for a life insurance policy until you receive an offer, which may be months after starting the process. Because people want to know what the cost will be, you have thousands of agents submitting dozens (or hundreds) of applications to multiple insurance companies every year. Of all the cases that an insurance company underwrites, it may only place five percent of the offers it makes. An insurance company has to perform 20 times the due diligence for each new customer. When you consider that many older applicants may have hundreds of pages of medical records (that must be reviewed to rate their health), it is clear that underwriting is a cumbersome, if not daunting, task.

In an attempt to streamline the underwriting process, companies use outsourced file reviewers in India, technology, and artificial intelligence to scan the volumes of medical records to find potential concerns. Once your application is "flagged" for a potential problem, it is difficult to convince overworked human underwriters that the problem is insignificant. The cost to being rated one or two classes higher could be as much as 50 percent additional mortality costs. Over the life of a $10,000,000 policy, that could result in hundreds of thousands of dollars in additional expense.

Even worse, if you are denied or rated for insurance, because your health records were unattractive to the underwriter, that fact is reported to the Medical Information Bureau ("MIB") and it follows you forever. It may be difficult to qualify for any insurance in the future.

To avoid these unnecessary risks, we hired a client underwriting advocate to work with our clients. This team of underwriters scans the clients' medical records before they are submitted to the insurance companies. If the advocate finds something troubling in the records, they advise the applicant to have a follow up appointment with the doctor or to get an additional test that may negate the red flag issue identified.

In the case of a complicated health situation for an applicant, the advocate will engage in preliminary discussions with the insurance company underwriters before they submit a formal application. That way, no client receives the dreaded "denial" that sits on their permanent record like a scarlet "D."

What does this cost? I pay the advocate a percentage of all the insurance business I place. This practice is beneficial in two ways. First, neither the clients nor my firm have to pay anything out of pocket for this valuable service. Second, the advocate is interested in seeing these policies placed because they earn part of the commission. Everyone wins in this scenario, and it's something you may want to consider yourself.

Mistake #2: Losing Half of Insurance Proceeds to Tax

Life insurance is highly recommended as a tool to support a family, or to pay the estate taxes due when you die. Insurance is attractive because the funds are available immediately to your survivors, without any delays of probate or expenses involved with liquidating assets as it may not be a good time to sell assets right after the owner dies. Despite the popularity of life insurance, most people own it incorrectly. This is even the case with highly educated physicians. A *Medical Economics* poll reported that 90 percent of doctors fail to utilize a simple legal tool that offers their families tremendous benefit.

Owning life insurance in your own name, in your spouse's name, jointly with a spouse, or in your living trust is a big mistake. All of these common ownership options will expose the cash value of the policy to your creditors and subject the death benefit proceeds to federal and state estate taxes (which could total 50 percent or more).

By utilizing an irrevocable trust, more specifically an Irrevocable Life Insurance Trust (ILIT), you can give your family a wide range of benefits, including:

- Protects your cash values from creditors
- Removes insurance proceeds from your estate
- Protects your children from lawsuits or divorce

This ILIT can be used to facilitate even more advanced estate planning beyond just life insurance – and it should only cost you a few thousand dollars to set up. A more advanced application of this technique is to have an ILIT own interests in a limited liability company (LLC) that owns the policy. This structure and all of its interesting corporate and family applications will be explained along the 5th Path.

Mistake #3: Using Life Insurance the Wrong Way

Like any product, business, employee, or even a garden, an insurance policy will do better if its reviewed and managed over time. Cash value insurance policies will have both expenses and credits every year. These expenses can be changed by the carrier each year. The credits are even more confusing as they are linked to either the insurance company's investment returns or the stock market.

Life insurance products never perform as illustrated, so you will want to review them every year to see if they require changes. Perhaps you missed a payment or two, expenses went up, or you suffered an unfavorable investment downturn. If you are slightly behind, you may find that adding a small amount of premium or slightly reducing the death benefit will significantly improve the policy performance or preserve the death benefit past your life expectancy.

Given that your agent probably did not shop every one of the thousands of potential policies before placing yours, you might find an exchange to another company's product might better suit your needs. How is this possible? One company may have lower mortality rates or may view your health more favorably. Another company may have a new product with lower expenses or different investment choices. Since there is no cost to reviewing your internal and external options, you should look closely at your policy every year or two.

Alternatively, your policy may be performing wonderfully, but your circumstances may have changed. Maybe you were using the life insurance for income protection, and now that your kids have grown, you want to use it for supplemental retirement. Perhaps, you bought a policy to save money tax-efficiently for retirement, and now you realize you have enough saved. This policy would be better suited as a death benefit policy for your children or grandchildren. You may have even purchased a policy as part of a buy-sell agreement, for key-man insurance, or as part of an executive compensation plan in your business – and now you plan to sell your company. These are opportunities for you to leverage this asset for your future needs.

Whether your situation and goals have changed or not, there are new product developments, changes in life expectancies and mortality costs, and changes in internal expenses to insurance policies every year. It makes sense to have a professional review of your existing policies and to shop for a one that fits your changing needs. If your health hasn't deteriorated considerably, you may be surprised how much you can save from having an "insurance physical."

Mistake #4: Cancelling Life Insurance the Wrong Way

Whether you are tired of paying premiums, or your situation has changed, at some point you may want to discontinue your life insurance policy. If you have a term policy, you can just stop paying. If you have a cash value policy, you can surrender the policy and retrieve your cash surrender value – this is the cash account value minus any surrender charges. Before you decide to walk down either of those paths, there is another option you may want to consider.

You Can Sell Your Life Insurance Policy

Though you may not be interested in exchanging your cash value and future premiums for a big death benefit in the future, there are people who are. Settlement companies specialize in raising funds from investors with long term investment horizons, and purchasing life insurance policies from individuals, trusts, or businesses. The settlement company pays you the agreed-upon sum for the policy and the company takes over all future premium payments. When you die, the company receives the death benefit.

What makes a settlement company interested in certain policies:

- Face value (death benefit) of $250,000 to $25,000,000
- Insured is 60 years old or older
- Insured of any age that is chronically or terminally ill
- Cash values are helpful, but not necessary.

According to the U.S. Government Accountability Office, payouts for life insurance settlements are often as low as 13 to 21 percent of the face value of the policy.

How Can You Get an Offer for Your Life Insurance Policy?

In order to sell a life insurance policy, you must find a buyer. We are happy to introduce you to a broker who specializes in life insurance policies, or you can look for a life settlement broker to find offers for your policy. Because the offers are very flexible, and subject to negotiation, we recommend you work with someone who has successfully performed this service for others and who has worked with multiple potential buyers (to get you the best price).

Once you find someone to represent you, they will ask for insurance policy documents and your medical records. Unlike your original underwriting experience, where you wanted the company to look favorably on your health, this exercise will prove more profitable for you when the insured is in poor health. After the potential buyers review the records, they may offer to purchase your policy. The price will primarily be based on:

- Your age and health status
- The policy type
- The cash account and cash surrender values of the policy
- Amount of future premiums projected

Prices will vary considerably. Generally speaking, prices for policies on older or terminally ill people or policies with very high death benefits are attractive to settlement companies because the opportunity for immediate or greater payout exist.

Buyer Beware: Pitfalls of Selling a Life Insurance Policy

If you can afford to keep paying your premiums and you have a spouse or dependents, you might be better off keeping your life insurance policy, seeking alternatives for your retirement or medical bills. The death benefit of your policy will always be more than what you will receive if you sell it. And be aware of these other pitfalls:

- **Tax consequences.** You may have to pay income and capital gains taxes. Be sure to talk to an accountant before making your decision.
- **Eligibility for benefits.** The cash gain from selling your policy may prohibit you from qualifying for Medicaid or other government benefits that you need.
- **Privacy concerns.** You will likely be required to share personal medical information in order to sell your life insurance policy. Settlement providers may frequently check up on your health status. Be sure to work with a trustworthy broker and settlement provider if you want to protect your privacy.
- **Roadblocks to other coverage.** If you sell your policy when you are older or have health problems, purchasing other life insurance coverage may be cost-prohibitive or impossible.
- **High-pressure tactics.** Be sure you work with a trustworthy broker who is licensed with your state insurance department. Don't fall prey to high-pressure sales tactics or a broker or provider who wants you to make a fast decision. If you can, work with the agent who sold you the policy, or ask your agent or financial advisor for a referral to a reputable settlement broker.

How do you know if you are getting a fair price? You could be selling yourself short by selling your policy. If the death benefit is significantly higher than what you are being offered, it might be best to hold on to the policy unless you absolutely need the funds and can no longer pay the premiums.

Also, be sure to pay attention to the fees being charged. You may have to surrender up to 30 percent of the proceeds to fees for the broker or other entities involved in the transaction.

If you do decide that selling a life insurance policy for cash is the right option for you, be sure to do your homework and shop around for the best offer. Don't take the first offer you get and remember that a higher selling price could actually bring you less cash if the fees are greater.

What Are Some Alternatives to Selling a Life Insurance Policy?
Life insurance settlement providers and brokers tout the practice as an acceptable estate planning tool. But in reality, it is a last-resort option that is only applicable in certain situations. You probably have a variety of other options to consider before you decide to sell your life insurance policy such as these:

- Borrow money from a cash-value life insurance policy. This is a tax-free option, and your life insurance policy stays in force.
- If you are terminally ill, find out if your term or permanent life insurance policy has an endorsement that allows you to access your death benefit early. This is a tax-free option that allows you to use your policy for expenses. Remember that the death benefit will be reduced by the amount that you withdraw early.

Charting a Better Path

Life insurance is an important piece of any financial plan. How you own life insurance can have a profound effect on how that insurance will benefit you, your family, or your business. If you make a mistake in the ownership of the policy, or you hastily transfer policy ownership, you could accidentally subject your family to income taxes, estate taxes, or both sets of taxes on the proceeds from your life insurance.

It is very important that you work with your team of advisors to determine how to utilize an insurance trust in your planning. Another way to own life insurance, and other assets, is in either a family limited partnership or a limited liability company. These tools will be discussed in the next chapter. For more detail about using insurance more effectively, download the **giraffeMONEY** ***Insurance Guide*** at www.GiraffeUniversity.com/resources.

Chapter 22
You Can Tame a Zebra – without Even Owning It

"I cannot always control what goes on outside.
But I can always control what goes on inside."
—Wayne Dyer

In our experience, it is not a lack of awareness of potential savings that stops wealthy families from tax planning. I have helped families transfer hundreds of millions of dollars with very little if any, tax liability. The economics of estate planning are not complicated in what my good friend Chris Erblich calls, "The Golden Age of Tax and Estate Planning." As an advisor to dozens of billionaire families, Chris says, "The big hurdle to gifting is the loss of control."

Families are concerned about spoiling their children by giving them too much, too soon, and are worried that they may themselves need the money later in life for some unfortunate shift in their business or investments. When they share these concerns, they are really saying they would like to be able to shift assets for income and estate tax benefits, but they don't want to give up control of the assets. Luckily, there are two ways to accomplish both considerations. We will discuss the first one in this chapter.

Limited Liability Companies Hold the Key

In the **giraffeMONEY** *Guide to Asset Protection* and the **giraffeMONEY** *Guide to Estate Planning*, there are detailed descriptions of family limited partnerships (FLPs) and limited liability companies (LLCs). Both of these tools are effective asset protection and tax-saving tools. They are interchangeable, but I will only mention the LLC to save time. LLCs offer spectacular estate tax benefits. Before I explain those, I want to show you how an LLC can save you tens of thousands of dollars in income taxes each year – which will more than offset any costs to create and manage them.

By gifting the LLC's interests to family members in lower marginal income tax brackets, you can effectively shift income through *income sharing.* A percentage of the income generated within the LLC will be taxed at the lower rates of the partners in lower marginal tax brackets. Typically, these are children or grandchildren. While the exact rules are more complex, generally, as long as the child is over 18 years of age, the child's share of the income will be taxed at a rate that is presumably lower than that of the working parents. Consider this example:

Case Study: Danny and Rina's LLC Reduces Taxes

Danny and Rina had annual taxable income of $100,000 from their rental real estate, which was worth $1 million. In a 40 percent combined state and federal income tax bracket, their total tax on this income came to $40,000. To reduce their taxes, they set up an LLC.

The LLC was funded with the real estate. Danny and Rina appointed themselves as managing members, so they retained 100 percent control. They gifted a 3 percent membership interest to each of their four children (Zach, Shiloh, Earvin, and Elgin) removing a total of 12 percent from the estate. Because each child's interest would be valued at about $20,000 (3 percent of $1 million, less the minority valuation discount), no gift tax applied to the transfers to the children. Danny and Rina made these 12 percent transfers to their children annually for five years.

Under the LLC agreement, the children were taxed on their share of the LLC's income; which, after five years, became 60 percent. In year five, 60 percent of the FLP's taxable income would be taxed at the children's lower tax rates. So, when the LLC assets earn $100,000 in income, 60 percent of that income was taxed at the children's rate—15 percent. Thus, their tax bill for operation of the LLC was $16,000 (40 percent on $40,000, the parents' share) plus $9,000 (15 percent on $60,000, the children's share).

Danny's family tax savings would be as follows:

Total tax with the LLC, year five:	$25,000
Total tax without the LLC, year five:	$40,000

Year five family income tax savings with the FLP: $15,000

Bear in mind that there were also savings in years one through four. Additionally, under the LLC agreement, the managing members did not have to distribute any LLC income to the members. This was totally within the discretion of Danny and Rina as managing members. Thus, Danny and Rina could pay all LLC taxes with the income and reinvest the remaining proceeds.

Estate Planning Benefits

Family limited partnerships and limited liability companies have three major benefits for estate planning. Let us examine each separately.

1. **Limited liability company assets avoid probate and continue.** Assets owned by your LLC do not go through probate. Only your interest in the LLC will. If you structure your LLC so that your intended beneficiaries eventually own most of the LLC interests by the time you die, beneficiaries will control the LLC assets or business while the probate process continues its deliberation. Because probate can last several years, this continued control can be crucial for operating a business or real estate interests.
2. **Limited liability companies utilize exemptions without giving up control.** An LLC has managing membership interests and membership interests. You can be the managing member of the LLC with only one percent of the total ownership – provided the one percent you own is 100 percent of the controlling interest. In this way, you control the assets, while 99 percent of the value can be outside your estate for estate tax purposes.
3. **Assets in limited liability companies may be worth less for tax purposes.** You may not want to gift your entire LLC interests during your lifetime, or it may be worth so much that the exemptions and annual gifts are not sufficient to remove everything you own from your taxable estate. If you die owning LLC interests, which are then subject to the estate tax, the

valuation given to those interests may be discounted and beneficial to you and your family.

Valuation Discounts for LLCs

The IRS recognizes that having a percentage ownership of an LLC that owns an asset is generally worth less than owning the asset outright. If you own a $20 bill and hold it at death, the IRS would assign an estate taxable value to that bill of $20. However, if you died owning a 20 percent interest in an LLC with four other family members—all with equal management rights and the LLC owned $100—the IRS may allow a valuation of your 20 percent interest well below $20. Here's why:

Lack of marketability discount. Unlike a $20 bill that can easily be used as $20, a 1/5 interest in an LLC is not marketable. You can't use it to buy gas or pay for parking. Even if someone recognized the value in the LLC, there is likely not much of a market for your 20 percent LLC interest when the other LLC members are all family members. Who would want to own part of an LLC worth $100 when the other owners are members of one family? What would an outsider pay for such an interest?

Minority interest discount. Because you own less than 50 percent of the LLC, the IRS will apply the minority ownership discount to your interest, unless you have retained most or all of the management rights. Having a 100 percent vote on how to spend $20 is worth a lot more than having a 1/5 vote on how to spend $100.

Tax-valuation discounts can be maximized by the proper drafting of the LLC agreement. Any provisions that restrict the transferability of LLC interests will weigh toward a higher lack of marketability discount. Likewise, clauses that limit the control of minority interest holders will substantiate greater minority ownership discounts. In this way, with proper drafting, LLCs can often enjoy valuation discounts of 20 to 30 percent or more. Imagine an estate worth $100 million which is owned in a series of well drafted LLCs. A reduction in value of $30 million could save a family almost $15 million in estate taxes and state inheritance taxes.

Charting a Better Path

The FLP and LLC are tremendous tools for asset protection, income tax, and estate planning. They are cornerstones of most planning for successful families and business owners. To learn more about how they can be structured for your benefit, you should review the **giraffeMONEY** ***Estate Planning Guide*** and the **giraffeMONEY** ***Asset Protection Guide*** at www.GiraffeUniversity.com/resources.

It is difficult to imagine how any plan for a Giraffe could be complete without multiple FLPs or LLCs. As you continue to the more complicated and powerful strategies in this book, you will see how LLCs are integral parts of an effective plan.

Chapter 23
A Giraffe Needs a Really Long Mirror

If you have ever tied a necktie, you may really appreciate this long introduction. Bear with me.

If a giraffe were to wear a necktie, where would he wear it? Does it go at the top of his neck near his head or at the bottom of his neck closer to his body?

I love that people get really excited about their answers to this question. A wild animal wearing a tie is even more preposterous than the ridiculous site of a dog in a sweater. It's not as ridiculous as the poor dog with the cone on its head, but at least that's functional. Nonetheless, the correct answer is the tie on the left – the low one.

What's more important than where the giraffe would place the tie is how the giraffe would actually put the tie on. If we can get past the lack of opposable thumbs, and the fact that their hip socket and knee joints won't let their legs come anywhere near their necks, we still have a much bigger hurdle. I was reminded while helping my son Tyler get dressed for his virtual high school graduation ceremony that I can't properly tie a tie without a mirror. Where the hell are we going to find an 20-foot tall mirror?

When it comes to a lack of an appropriate mirror, it is the same problem we had for decades. with estate planning and asset protection. There have always been one-way financial transfers to provide benefits, but those always left one spouse in a precarious position. For example, a spouse in a high liability profession (obstetrician, real estate developer, giraffe mirror installer, etc.) could gift her shares to a trust for her husband and children. This would protect the family's wealth from her liability, but there is a big problem. She no longer owns those assets.

From an estate tax perspective, there has always been a similar dilemma. Each spouse has a unified credit. This is the amount that a spouse can leave to heirs (during one's lifetime or at death) without federal estate taxes. Currently, that amount is $11,580,000 per person. The problem has always been that the exemption is not portable. That means that, although you can leave an unlimited amount of wealth to your spouse without tax, you do not transfer your "get out of taxes free" card along with the assets. This created additional planning difficulties.

Alternatively, there has always been an array of techniques to move money from a taxable estate down to the next generation. In fact, in a low interest rate environment like we have today, it's very easy to remove $50 to $100 million out of an estate with very little friction. Removing large estate values is not the problem. The challenge was always that the success of these techniques was predicated on the irrevocable transfer to the next generation. It has been very difficult for one spouse to retain access and nearly impossible for both spouses to have access to the money. The "reflection" of the wealth between spouses or from one generation to another was simply nonexistent.

Look! A Fun House (with high ceilings)

At least twice in the last 10 years, we faced major changes in estate tax laws. First, the Bush tax cuts called for a complete repeal of the estate tax. That was only going to be for one year, 2010. Estate taxes were schedule to come back in 2011. Right before that took place, on December 17, 2010, President Obama signed into law the Tax Relief, Unemployment Insurance Reauthorization, and Job Creation Act of 2010 (the "Act"). In general, the Act provides tax relief for gift, estate and generation-skipping transfer (GST) tax purposes by lowering tax rates and increasing tax exemptions. This act gave us fantastic estate planning benefits, but the gift (pun intended) was short-lived and scheduled to sunset two years later. In both "sunset" situations, the savvy affluent made estate planning top priority.

> **Timing is Everything**
> A Client of mine owns a very large national company. During that short window when there was amazing estate planning leverage, they were able to move 99 percent of their net worth out of their estate through a strategy similar to the one you will see in this chapter. Now, less than 10 years later, they have a company worth almost $100,000,000 and a taxable estate of significantly less than $5 million. They took advantage of the crazy situation and you should too.

If you want crazy and unpredictable, 2020 will give you that. Regardless of who wins the 2020 Presidential election and how the balance of Senate and House land, it's virtually certain that tax rates will go up. We cannot create trillions of dollars of losses and stimulus packages and not pay for them. Given the expected turmoil and uncertainty, you have to accept a very serious possibility that some of today's amazing tax benefits will disappear. We currently have the most flexible and easiest to negotiate set of rules this country has seen in more than 40 years. Before things get too wacky and it's too late, you must take advantage of the most amazing (and easy) estate planning tool I've ever seen.

The Incredible Shrinking Giraffe?

In light of the significant potential for major change, you must consider creating an Intentionally Defective Irrevocable Trust ("IDIT") as soon as possible. By creating his and hers IDITs and gifting assets to those IDIT, you can fully utilize your $23,160,000 of combined gift tax exemptions. Even if you are not worth $23 million, you would utilize the IDIT for as much as you do have. How can I say this with such conviction? Take a look for yourself:

Description of His and Hers IDIT Strategy

- An IDIT is an irrevocable trust. The assets are not subject to any of your creditors.
- Assets transferred to the IDIT, and their appreciation from the time you transfer them until you die, should not be subject to estate taxes when you die.
- The assets of the IDIT should not be subject to creditor or divorce claims of any of your beneficiaries — like children or grandchildren.
- An IDIT is designed to receive gifts from you or to borrow funds from you to make investments on behalf of your descendants. The Trustee (who can be your spouse) will use the trust assets for the benefit of the beneficiaries during their lifetimes.

More than 7 Years of GOOD LUCK — This Mirror isn't Breaking

- **Your Spouse May be a Beneficiary of IDIT.** Depending on the assets transferred to the IDIT, your spouse may be a beneficiary of the IDIT for your children. Your spouse may also serve as the Trustee or Co-Trustee of the IDIT, controlling assets he/she may also use for health, education, maintenance and support in the accustomed manner of living.
- **Spouse May Create Similar IDIT.** In addition to an IDIT established for the benefit of your spouse and descendants, your spouse may create a similar IDIT for the benefit of you and your descendants and fund this IDIT with her remaining gift tax exemption.
- Many clients prefer to establish two IDITs (one for each spouse). This structure allows each spouse access to the assets of his or her respective IDIT while providing the other benefits explained in this chapter.

Potential Risks of Using an IDIT

The amazing attorneys I work with to implement very impactful strategies are adamant that clients understand every possibly risk. I appreciate this about them, so I agreed to share the four risks they insist clients be aware of while contemplating this and any other estate planning technique. Below the risks, I have added a list of the practical impacts and the workarounds we use to easily mitigate each of these risks.

1. **An IDIT is an irrevocable trust,** and as such, any gift to it cannot be undone.
    a. **Reality 1:** You aren't losing anything. If you and your spouse split up your community property, and give it to each other's IDIT, you two collectively still have control and access to all of your assets.
    b. **Reality 2:** There isn't much inconvenience or cost to this irrevocable gift.
2. **Divorce.** Gifts you make to the IDIT for your spouse or your children cannot be reacquired.
    a. **Reality 1**: If you and your spouse held your assets jointly and did not implement this strategy, the court would divvy up your assets in a divorce.
    b. **Reality 2**: A future divorce would actually be much less contentious and less expensive because the assets would already have been separated and gifted.
3. **Death.** When your spouse dies, the trust you created for your spouse, children, and grandchildren would become for the benefit of the children (or other named remainder beneficiaries). You would not have access to that half of your assets.
    a. **Reality 1:** This one is real. You may need to have access to more than your half of the estate to cover your living expenses, but it is easily managed.
    b. **Reality 2:** To hedge against this risk and to provide additional liquidity for the surviving spouse, life insurance is often purchased on each spouse. You would hold insurance on your spouse in the trust you can access. Your spouse would own a policy on you in the trust she can access. This easily eliminates this problem.
4. **Reciprocal Trusts.** We must be careful to create trusts that do not violate the "reciprocal trust" doctrine which would negate some of the benefits.
    a. **Reality 1:** Trusts must not be exact mirror images of one another and must have differences that would allow the IRS

to determine that your economic positions were different before and after the gifts.

b. **Reality 2:** This is easily managed by seasoned attorneys. I work with such attorneys who are licensed to work in at least 40 states. If you would like a referral, please contact me at www.chrisjarvis.com/contact.

How One Family Turned $34,000 into $74,000,000

To show you the power of this particular solution, we have shared slightly modified details of a particular client's situation. Here are the assumptions:

a. Husband and wife have $20,000,000 of assets in their taxable estate.
b. Assets are expected to grow at 10 percent per year (after tax).
c. Joint life expectancy is approximately 20 years.
d. The couple wants to protect those funds from lawsuits and eliminate unnecessary estate tax liabilities.
e. They want to retain access to these funds during their lifetime.
f. They want to protect their children's inheritances from divorce, but don't want to have to risk the relationships with their children or in-laws by asking for prenuptial or postnuptial agreements.

We calculated the impact the planning could offer them. We assumed the projected combined federal estate tax and state inheritance taxes would be 55 percent. You could look at this estimate as the highest federal estate rate in the last 20 years. Alternatively, you could support this estimate with today's low 40 percent estate tax rate and a 15 percent state inheritance tax rate (the highest in any state is now 18 percent). Of course, it is uncertain when the clients will die, and we can't know what the combined tax rate will be at that time.

After meeting with the lawyers and with our team to discuss the plan and the potential benefits (which you will see shortly), the clients decided to move forward with the IDIT transaction. The process took less than 90 days. Here are the steps they took:

a. Each spouse created an IDIT for the benefit of the other spouse and the children. The terms of the two trusts were substantially different enough to be compliant with IRS guidelines.

c. The husband made a gift of $10,000,000 of separate property to the IDIT for wife, children and future grandchildren.
d. The wife made a gift of $10,000,000 of separate property to the IDIT for husband, children, and small amounts for cousins.
e. The clients moved existing life insurances on each other to the proper trusts.
f. The clients filed gift tax returns, utilized most of their $23 million exemption, paid $0 tax, and removed all of these assets from their estate.
g. Total fees for planning, legal structures, and gift tax returns were $34,000.

Potential Results at Time of Second Death

With HIS and HERS IDIT	$134,550,000 net to heirs
Without IDIT Planning	$60,547,500 net to heirs
Value of IDIT Planning	**$74,002,500 net to heirs**

By spending a couple of months in the planning, and less than $34,000, the clients created the creditor protection they desired, protected their kids and grandkids from unnecessary taxes and the threat of divorce, and enhanced their total estate by $74,000,000.

Charting a Better Path

Along the 6th Path, you will learn how to avoid conflicts of interest with your advisors, but the IDIT has no conflict. I am not an attorney and I have no financial incentive to send you to a law firm to create this IDIT structure. If you do utilize this technique, you will remove up to $23 million and all of its future growth from your taxable estate. This will save you money you might otherwise pay me to help you transfer in the future. Despite a perceived conflict of interest that I might have to recommend this strategy to you, I am begging you to seriously consider this technique. It is the easiest, quickest, most impactful solution you can use to take a huge dent out of the friction you will encounter when trying to pass wealth to the next generation.

The his and hers IDIT allows you to remove $23 million from your taxable estate while still having access to those funds. The technique protects those assets from any creditors you and your spouse may have. It also protects all of the growth of those assets from both estate taxes and creditors. This truly is a get out of taxes free card that should save your family up to $10 million dollars. If you only acted on one thing in this entire book, this is one of three strategies that deserves very serious consideration.

5th PATH
Teach It to Plant and Feed It for a Lifetime

You already know that the giraffe is very different from all the other migrating animals. We touched on the benefits of their dietary differences earlier, but it gets even more interesting. As a quick review, giraffes eat the leaves from trees, rather than the grass that every other animal on the plains seeks. This doesn't just save the giraffe from competition with the millions of zebra, wildebeest and buffalo. Because trees can access water under the soil, they grow in places that are too dry (on the surface) for grass to grow. This allows the giraffe two distinct advantages over other animals:

1) Giraffes face less competition — as they feed in different places
2) Giraffe have more freedom — they can survive and thrive in more places.

Think about your business and your personal financial situation. How much would you enjoy facing less competition? How beneficial would it be for you to enter new markets?

Have you ever felt trapped in a job? Maybe you felt like you were stuck working with a customer, supplier, or vendor? How would it feel to have the freedom to quit your job and follow your dream? I have asked many clients these questions, but it wasn't until I asked myself these same questions that my life changed. In 2014, I decided to prepare my company for sale. By the end of 2016, I had signed the paperwork on a multimillion-dollar sale that helped me get out of doing things I didn't enjoy so I could focus on the things I love doing now. If you want to watch Jack Canfield (author of Chicken Soup for the Soul) interview me about my path to selling my company, you can watch it at www.GiraffeUniversity.com/company.

Visualize how amazing it would feel to let go of a problematic employee, fire a challenging customer, sever an unhealthy relationship, or discontinue a struggling product with no worry whatsoever. Let's dive deeper into how giraffes *feed differently* to learn an invaluable lesson.

Most animals have a one-way relationship with their food. Predators play a simple "zero-sum" game where there is one winner and one loser. Lions, cheetah, hyenas, leopards, and wild dogs hunt animals for food. The ones they catch die, so that the predators can live. Herbivores, not called giraffes, are not that different. When you see herd migrate into a plain, they stay until the grass is gone —completely. Then, they move on to greener pastures (literally). The grass is not gone forever, but it will not sprout again until the new rains come.

The giraffe has a symbiotic relationship with its favorite food source — the acacia tree. Also known as the giraffe thorn or camel thorn tree, the acacia grows thorns that can be over 3 inches long. The giraffe uses its 18-inch tongue to navigate around the thorns to access its tasty leaves, but the acacia does have a plan B. When these leaves are pulled from the tree, the acacia releases tannins. These water-soluble, carbon-based compounds have many uses for humans, helping us make leather, wine and cocoa. The giraffe is far less appreciative of the tannins. Not only do they taste awful, the tannins also interfere with digestive enzymes and bind to consumed plant proteins in the giraffe – making food very difficult to digest. Giraffes quickly learn that the bad taste and stomach cramps go together – so they move on to another tree.

When the bitter tannins of the acacia tree are also released into the air, it doesn't just spread to the rest of the tree. The tannins travel downwind as far as 50 yards. When other acacia trees receive the message, they heed its silent warning cry and emit their own tannins. This causes the giraffe to move upwind, away from the tannin forest, to find trees that have not yet caught wind (pun intended) of the giraffe's plan. This allows the tree to survive and provide food for other giraffes in the future, but it gets even more interesting.

The acacia's defense teaches the giraffe to walk upwind as it searches for more food. By walking upwind, the giraffe is alerted to the scent of predators in its path. If it walked in the opposite direction, the scent of the giraffe would be telegraphed to nearby lions who would be happy to wait in ambush. The acacia tree and giraffe work together in a way that helps both survive AND this helps preserve other acacia trees and giraffes as well. There is simply no such symbiotic relationship that works within a species, across to its flora food source, then across its flora. I find it truly amazing.

Think of yourself as the giraffe and your investments and business as the acacia tree. Along the first two paths, you learned how hard it is to make money. On the last two paths saw ways to preserve that hard-earned wealth. Next, you will see how to get the most out of your investments by putting time and money into real estate, securities, and other businesses so that you don't have to work so hard. There are only so many hours in the day, and limited days for you to spend with your kids, family, and friends. You must use them wisely.

When you start thinking of ways to make every investment more like the giraffe-acacia relationship, you will see a better path. This path will lead to many sales and referrals from every client and will net multiple benefits from each relationship. This amazing leverage will help you get so much more out of what you do, so you can do more with what you have.

Chapter 24
What Came First, the Giraffe or the Egg?

Created by Laura Lin from Noun Project

Ok, that's a trick question. Giraffes don't lay eggs but imagine how big they would be! Like all mammals, giraffes have live births. We will describe this in detail at the trailhead of the 7th Path but suffice it to say that it is an exceedingly more abrupt and traumatic entrance to the world than breaking out of an egg. Let's pivot to the giraffe's obvious cousin, the chicken, for this chapter's lesson.

What came first: the chicken or the egg? This is the classic "causality dilemma." This becomes a dilemma when you realize that either answer could be correct. Did something other than a chicken lay an egg that developed into a chicken? Did a chicken lay the first egg as a different form of reproduction? Questions like this one take the researchers, the curious and the argumentative down a path of *causality*. Did the chicken cause the creation of eggs, or did an egg cause the creation of chickens?

You don't have to be a Beatle to be an egg man (or a walrus). Some scientists contend that the egg must have come first. There were direct ancestors of the modern chicken that did indeed produce eggs. Perhaps, enough genetic mutations created the first modern chicken – from two non-chicken parents.

On the other hand, the sky is not falling if you have a different opinion. My not-so-little chicken is my twelve-year-old daughter, Chloe. She was only nine when she overheard me discussing this idea for my book, ***6 Secrets to Leveraging Success: A Guide for Entrepreneurs, Family Offices, and Their Trusted Advisors***. She quickly jumped in and said,

"There's no dilemma. God created all the animals, including the chickens. The chicken came first." Many people over the age of nine also believe the concept of creationism.

In the third camp, we all know very intelligent and well-read friends who love to show off their debate (argument) skills (wouldn't you agree, George Peng?). These pains-in-the-ass think that the dilemma is merely a question of semantics, rather than one of biology. They say that, since the chicken is mentioned before the egg, the answer is simply the chicken came before the egg.

You may be wondering what *caused* me to include a "chicken and egg" piece in a book about giraffes and money. You may be asking yourself if this chapter is the *effect* of an exhausted or hallucinogenic author's attempt to get the book to his publisher on time. Rest assured, those concerns need not be mutually exclusive. If you indulge me, I will make a connection between the chicken and the egg question, and a very popular theory about money. Since money is the unit of measurement for income and wealth, it is often a proxy for success.

What comes first, Having or Making money?

Like the chicken and the egg, the "having" versus "making" money question is another causality dilemma. Most people can appreciate that both could come first. Let's look at some direct and indirect ways that each of these two answers can be correct before we offer suggestions for leveraging your situation.

Let's start with the oldest recorded way to "have" money – through an inheritance. This was seen along the 4th Path. Monarchies would leave wealth and power to the next generation. Having a crown, a treasure chest, and an army seemed like one hell of a head start. Contrast a royal upbringing to that of a peasant family. Royals contemplate how to take over new lands or how to open valuable trade routes with the East. The working class must get up early and work their farms from dawn to dusk to be able to feed the family and pay the tariffs. They were so busy that they had precious little time for planning. The only opportunity for leverage was the dream of one day having oxen to help with the heavy workload.

Though the challenges of the poor haven't changed much, the opportunities for leveraging money certainly have. You don't need to be given a kingdom to get a head start. There are many ways that successful families can, and do, help their children. The good old-fashioned inheritance is an obvious one. According to research by the Spectrem Group, as cited by Bloomberg, over 73 percent of surveyed investors under age fifty with assets above $25 million told the group that inheritance factored into their success. Long before the inheritance, families who "have money" generally afford their children a superior education. This can lead to higher paying jobs and increased opportunities for professional advancement. With greater income, the children will *make* more money. All things being equal, earning more will cause them to eventually *have* even more.

You have undoubtedly heard the phrase, "It takes money to make money." This adage appears to be a universally accepted. The phrase supports the idea that you must "have money" to be able to "make money." The questions that anyone seeking to earn more money should be asking are:

1) How important is it to save and reinvest my earnings?
2) What can I do if I am not making much money now?

In this chapter, I will prove (mathematically) that having money does in fact allow you to make *more* money. More importantly, you will learn how your money will make you more money as you climb each rung of the socio-economic ladder.

While everyone with a Twitter handle or YouTube channel hopes to break the internet with excess traffic, mathematicians dream of gaining notoriety from breaking (disproving) a universally accepted theorem or law. Those exceptions to the rule (that you must first have money to make money) could be the keys to unlocking the wealthiest Americans' secrets to success.

Spoiler Alert: if there weren't ways to make money without first having money, there wouldn't be many pages in this book!

How Much Money Do Americans Make?

As a mathematician, I pride myself on making sure that the numbers I share are accurate. Luckily, I turned to a longtime friend, Dr. Axel Anderson, Professor of Economics at Georgetown, a classmate from Classical High School (Providence, RI). Dr. Anderson pointed me to the award-winning research of Emmanuel Saez, Professor of Economics at Berkeley.

Before we dive into Dr. Saez' research, the most detail-oriented of you may notice that the numbers below are slightly different from what was shared in the opening chapters. There is a good explanation. First, the information in the opening chapters represents an updated view of the current state of wealth in America. Second, Dr. Saez's numbers reported below are unmodified. His data and analysis earned him international acclaim and the Clark Medal in Economics. I dare not threaten the integrity of his work by attempting to change it. With that, let's consider the following:

Income Distribution (Including Realized Capital Gains)

Percentile threshold (1)	Income threshold (2)	Income Groups (3)	Number of families (4)	Average income in each group (5)
Bottom 90%	$0	Bottom 90%	150,582,600	$34,074
Top 10%	$124,810	Top 10 - 1%	15,058,260	$195,709
Top 1%	$442,900	Top 1 - 0.1%	1,505,826	$765,815
Top 0.1%	$2,045,000	Top 0.1 - 0.01%	150,583	$3,984,218
Top 0.01%	$11,267,000	Top 0.01%	16,731	$31,616,431
		Total	*167,314,000*	*$61,920*

Let's start by explaining what this chart is telling us. Columns 1 and 2 go together. As an example, only ten percent of American families earn more than $124,810. Only one percent of American families (one out of every 100) earn more than $442,900 per year. Only 0.01 percent (one in 10,000 families) earn more than $11,267,000 per year. As you can see, the income numbers increase substantially with each jump.

Columns 3, 4 and 5 should be evaluated together. This is an ingenious dissection of data by Dr. Saez. He is considering the bottom 90 percent of each grouping, so he can eliminate any distortion in the data that may result from the inclusion of the very high earners in the group. Consider the following: Bill Gates and nine schoolteachers are standing together on stage. I could say that the average net worth of the group was approximately $9 billion. That would be accurate, but very misleading. You might think that all ten were billionaires, but the reality is that Bill Gates is worth $87 billion.

Let's examine the Top ten percent row in the table above. Column 3 is titled "Top 10%- 1%." That should read "top ten percent minus the top one percent." This group includes families who earn more than $124,910 per year but excludes the top ten percent of that group, who earn more than $442,900. This is a group of 15 million families with an average income of $195,709. If you examine the next row, labeled "Top 1% - top 0.1%". There are over 1.5 million families earning more than $442,900 and less than $2,045,000 per year. The average income of this group is $765,815.

Please bear with me. I promise there won't be a test. You don't need to understand how to create the tables. Once we get through two more short tables, you may not even need to understand the entire tables. I will call out all the important observations that are necessary to make my point. That being said, what are the big takeaways from the chart above?

First, the average American family earns $61,920 per year. This number is italicized in the last row and last column of the table. Many successful people I know think $62,000 is a modest, but livable income. I must confess that even I, as a mathematician who should have known better, fell victim to the data distortion trap. I blindly accepted the average income number to reflect the "average" American family's earnings. I have quoted that average income to my children on numerous occasions to demonstrate that our lives are privileged and something to be appreciated. My kids gave those conversations as much credence as I gave my father's "I walked five miles to school in the snow, uphill both ways" stories.

When I looked at the data from Dr. Saez, I was shocked to see the impact the top ten percent of earners had on the data. In the top line of data in the table, you can see that the bottom 90 percent of American families earns an average of $34,074. I found that number to be disturbingly low. I don't know anyone who believes $34,000 is a reasonable income. I am not going to jump into a discussion about income inequality in America. That is not the topic for this book. I merely share this example to show you how "average income" statistics can be very misleading when you include outliers. Removing those outliers will help you gain a better appreciation for what is actually happening behind the data.

Second, take a look at the income numbers at the higher end of the table. In the row titled "Top 1%," you will see that only one in 100 families (there are over 1.5 million of them) earn more than $442,900 per year. Further, only one in ten of those who earn more than $442k will earn over

$2M per year. Those are the 0.1 percent. The target market for this book are the one percent who earn more than $442k who want to become even more successful. Let's learn how to do that.

How Much Does It *Really* Take to Make More Money?

The previous table included taxable income: earned income, passive investment income, and realized capital gains (assets sold for a profit or loss). Dr. Saez went a step further and removed the investments gains from the table. Below, you will see how much income is generated from labor and passive investments in each class.

Income Distribution (Excluding Realized Capital Gains)

Percentile threshold (1)	Income threshold (2)	Income Groups (3)	Number of families (4)	Average income in each group (5)
Bottom 90%	$0	Bottom 90%	150,582,600	$33,219
Top 10%	$121,810	Top 10 - 1%	15,058,260	$187,226
Top 1%	$407,760	Top 1 - 0.1%	1,505,826	$670,188
Top 0.1%	$1,635,100	Top 0.1 - 0.01%	150,583	$2,906,694
Top 0.01%	$7,474,600	Top 0.01%	16,731	$18,862,641
		Total	*167,314,000*	*$57,281*

Unsurprisingly, the second chart has lower numbers than the first chart because realized capital gains were removed. I won't waste your time summarizing this table like I did with the previous one – partly because I don't want to bore you and partly because I'm running out of space in this chapter. What is more important for all of us to consider is what was removed from the previous table to generate this one. The difference between the numbers in the two tables is the investment gain for each group. This is the value that the extra earned money, reinvested for the families' benefit, has earned for its owners. Consider the following:

Realized Capital Gains (aka Investment Income) by Group

Percentile threshold	Average income in each group	Realized Capital Gains	Cap Gains as % of Income	Capital Gains as Multiple of Bottom 90% Income
(1)	(2)	(3)	(4)	(5)
Bottom 90%	$33,219	$855	2.6%	0.026
Top 10%	$187,226	$8,463	4.5%	0.26
Top 1%	$670,188	$95,627	14.3%	2.9
Top 0.1%	$2,906,694	$1,077,524	37.1%	32.4
Top 0.01%	$18,862,641	$12,753,790	67.6%	384.9
Total	*$57,281*	*$4,639*	*8.1%*	

So, not only does income grow exponentially as you move into the higher threshold, but the investment income grows. Look at the top one percent as an example. That group earns $95,627 of realized capital gains. That is 14.3 percent more income, above their active income, each year. 14.3 percent may not sound like much, but it equates to almost three years of pretax income for the average family in the bottom 90 percent. THAT is a lot of money. Imagine how much easier your life could be if you had three additional years of income this year!

If you look at top 0.1 percent, the level of income that only one in 1,000 people will achieve, the numbers are staggering. That group of people earns nearly $3M per year. In addition, they earn over $1M per year in capital gains. The investment amount, which is symbolic of the profit they have earned on their savings, is equivalent to 32.4 years of income for the average family in the bottom 90 percent.

How to Interpret Income Percentile Charts

Category	How many Americans reach this level?
Bottom 90%	This group represents the 9 out of 10 people who didn't reach the next level (the top 10% of earners).
Top 10%	1 out of every 10 people will reach this level.
Top 1%	1 out of every 100 people will reach this level.
Top 0.1%	1 out of every 1,000 people will reach this level.
Top 0.01%	1 out of every 10,000 people will reach this level.

Charting a Better Path

The higher income families boost their incomes significantly (37 to 67 percent) through their investments. Contrast that to the 99 percent of Americans who earn less than five percent of their income from their investments. Think of earning money as the chicken and investing money as the egg. You can't be 100 percent sure which one must come first, but you do understand that the more you earn, the more you can invest. You also understand that the more investments you make, the more likely you are to earn more. Don't think of this as a vicious cycle. Think of Einstein (and his vicious hair).

In Einstein's later years of life, he was asked, "What is the most powerful force on earth?" He responded, "The power of compound interest!" The more you earn, the more you can save. The more you save, the more you can invest. The more you invest, the more it compounds into a legacy. The numbers we just shared from Dr. Saez prove this point decades later. How could anyone possibly argue that money doesn't help you earn more money?

Chapter 25
Take Giraffe Yoga — for Your Whiplash

"The key is for the audience to never know,
so I have a plan B for every illusion."
— David Copperfield

A giraffe has a 6-foot-long neck, but size isn't the only problem here. The giraffe has to stretch its neck up to eat, down to drink, and is constantly looking around to survey its situation. On top of that, males battle for mating rights by striking each other with their necks. Interestingly, the giraffe has the same number of vertebrae as a human. The only difference is those seven vertebrae are much larger and further apart than ours. In addition to the "pains in the neck" we all have, the neck is the focal point for everything that makes a giraffe a giraffe. It simply can't afford to be in traction.

Your wealth may seem a lot like the giraffe's neck. There are so many different planning areas and countless tools and strategies to consider. You have investments, taxes, lawsuits, estate planning, retirement, insurance – and you may be running a business too. Each one of these areas has the potential to pull you in a different direction. If you aren't careful, obsession with one area of planning could pull you completely out of alignment.

Along the 2nd Path, you learned that leverage is of the utmost importance in building wealth. In the last chapter, you saw the importance of investing to create leverage of time, effort and money. Wealthy people use other people's efforts to make them a much larger percentage of their income than hard workers do. Now, we need to add another important concept for your investment strategy: flexibility.

You need to leverage your time, your money, your mental capacity, and the professionals on your team. The best way to do this is to "kill two birds with one stone," and address multiple concerns at one time. This may mean:

1. Addressing two or three current planning concerns with one strategy or solution

2. Implementing a strategy that can be modified ***<u>when</u>*** circumstances or needs change

Double (or Triple) Your Pleasure

Along the prior path, you read about "Taming a Zebra – without Even Owning It." The chapter was about the limited liability company (LLC) and the Family Limited Partnership (FLP). You saw those tools offer convenient ways to protect real estate, brokerage accounts, and even assets of your company. You also saw by gifting interests in those two entities, you can maintain the control of the asset while potentially lowering both your family's current income tax and its future estate tax. The elegance of the LLC and FLP is they can do all of these tricks at once. You don't have to give up one benefit for the others.

At the end of the last path, you read about the spectacular His and Her IDIT solution. This is a perfect example of a very flexible tool that offers great leverage. You can eliminate over $11 million of gift or estate tax, protect over $23 million from lawsuits, and protect your children and grandchildren from divorce. Further on this path, you will come across the TrEE program. This solution helps business owners transform employee expenses into equity for the owner. It creates tax-free retirement income, enhances the value of a company (before sale), and offers additional protection to the company.

When, Not If

In the second bullet point, you may have noticed the word ***<u>when</u>*** was italicized, underlined and in bold. Perhaps you have heard the phrases *life is plan B* or *life happens.* In 25 years of experience, meeting thousands of wealthy business owners and families, I can tell you one thing with absolute certainty. No plan my firms have ever created went according to plan. Zero.

Life will always throw you a series of curveballs. Like in baseball, you don't know what off speed pitch you might see, and you certainly don't know when it might come. At 40 years old, I had a young daughter, owned a successful financial company, earned over $600,000 per year, and everyone in my family was healthy. Over the last ten years, I have been through a divorce, lost my younger sister, had both parents and one of my in-laws diagnosed with incurable cancer, lost my mother-in-law (who didn't have cancer) and just lost my father this month. I have also been kicked out of

TWO companies I started, been in multiple expensive lawsuits, and almost filed bankruptcy. Shit definitely happens!

At 40, I had a lot of plans. Other than being alive today, none of them happened as I expected. On a positive note, I would have gone bankrupt (not good for a financial advisor) had it not been for a client and friend who invested in me and my new business. I have since built that company and sold it for millions of dollars. I have remarried and adopted two stepchildren. Both my parents were still alive. This book and Giraffe University have been a source of great fun for me. I share my story to emphasize that I have not only seen how things don't go according to plan, but I have also lived it myself.

Charting a Better Path

Along the 2nd Path, you saw the importance of leverage in accumulating wealth. The goal of leverage is to create efficiency. In wealth accumulation, it means earning more with less effort. The same leverage concept is applied to the implementation of planning solutions. If you utilize a tool that offers numerous benefits, you add flexibility and efficiency to your planning. Being able to use something you already have is much faster, easier, and cheaper than going out and researching something new to build or buy. There are both legal and financial vehicles that offer extraordinary leverage and flexibility. Let's explore them next.

Chapter 26
Buy a Swiss Army *Life*?

"A fool thinks himself to be wise,
but a wise man knows himself to be a fool."
—William Shakespeare

You already know about the leverage of life insurance. You pay a small premium each year, and your heirs will receive a large death benefit when you pass. This is why life insurance is used by families for income replacement and to cover the estate taxes due at death. Businesses utilize policies for buy sell agreements and key-man insurance to protect the company.

Would you be surprised to learn that the wealthiest families and most successful businesses in America use life insurance for completely different reasons? In this chapter, you will see how properly structured and maintained life insurance products can offer those benefits and many, many more. The flexibility of life insurance is based on four key characteristics. Once you understand these, you will see how the more powerful strategies I will introduce later could help your family and your business.

Characteristics that Make Insurance So Valuable

Life insurance has many characteristics and offers various benefits. Savvy investors take advantage of life insurance as an investment because it is a flexible planning tool that will help address many planning challenges in an efficient way. The following attributes make Cash Value Life Insurance (CVLI) a valuable investment and therefore, capture the interest of successful investors:

1. *Amounts in life insurance policies grow tax-deferred.* While investments outside of retirement plans and life insurance policies are taxed on income and realized capital gains, funds within a CVLI policy grow completely tax-free. This is why life insurance is attractive as a wealth-accumulation and tax-reduction vehicle. It is viewed

as an unlimited after-tax retirement plan by our wealthiest clients.

2. *Account balance values in life insurance policies can be accessed tax free at any time.* When you take funds out of a retirement plan (pension or individual retirement account [IRA]), these withdrawals are always subject to income tax and may be subject to a penalty if withdrawn before age 59½. With a CVLI policy, you can take tax-free loans against the cash value at any time. There is never a tax penalty and there is no tax on the loan as long as you keep the policy in force and the policy is not a modified endowment contract (MEC).
3. *Life insurance is asset protected.* All 50 states give some measure of asset protection to CVLI policies. Thus, this asset can play a role in your asset-protection plan. Working with your advisory team, you can determine how best to leverage the rules in your state.
4. *Life insurance has beneficial tax valuation.* In dealing with the 70 percent-plus tax trap facing pensions and IRAs, life insurance can play a valuable role. The essence of this rule is that life insurance enables the plan owner, who would otherwise lose 70 percent of his plan holdings to estate and income taxes, to pass 100 percent of those dollars and more to heirs.

As you see, life insurance offers many benefits to the policy owners. It can grow tax free, provide a tax-advantaged death benefit, and is protected from lawsuit creditors. This flexibility is what allows the successful investors to use life insurance to meet their planning challenges more efficiently.

The Unlimited After-tax Retirement Plan

Along the 4th Path, we explained how successful investors maximize their use of retirement plans. A major concern is the contribution limits of these plans don't allow giraffe earners to save enough to sustain their quality of life in retirement. The federal government came up with a great alternative plan for taxpayers, called the Roth IRA. This IRA is different from qualified retirement plans because there is no tax deduction for your contributions. The Roth IRA allows you to make after tax contributions with the privilege of never paying tax on growth or on withdrawals after age 59 ½. This is a fantastic news – except successful people can't use the Roth IRA. First, the contribution limits are only $6,000 per year ($7,000 if you are 50+) and you are disqualified if you are an individual earning more than $124,000 or married filing jointly earning $196,000 in 2020.

When you compare the Roth IRA to cash value life insurance, you will see some key similarities:

	Roth IRA	Cash Value Life Insurance
Annual Contribution	$6,000	$6,000,000
Income Limits	$124,000 Single $196,000 Married	$124,000,000 Single $196,000,000 Married
Tax on Earnings	Tax-Free	Tax-Free
Withdrawals	Tax-Free (after Age 59 ½)	Tax-Free (No Age Limit)
Value to Heirs at Death	Account Value 100%	Death Benefit 100% to 10,000%
Ownership Restrictions	Individuals	Individuals, Trusts, LLCs, FLPs, and Corporations

When compared with a Roth IRA, the benefits of life insurance are that the annual premiums are practically unlimited, and the funds can be accessed before age 59½. CVLI can also be owned by a company or transferred to a trust to manage estate planning or creditor protection concerns. These benefits make CVLI a very attractive alternative or complement to retirement plans.

Leveraging the Ultimate Leverage Tool

Real estate developers use leverage all the time. They borrow other people's money for the majority of the expenses for their projects. Though they have very little of their own money invested, they keep all the profit after paying back the lender (plus interest). Like real estate, savvy investors have taken advantage of what is called *premium financing*—using other people's money to buy much greater amounts of life insurance than they could afford on their own.

How do you think banks make money? The answer is simple: They borrow money from people through deposits, certificates of deposit, checking and savings accounts, and so on. They lend money to people to buy homes or cars or to start businesses. Because they may only pay you one to two percent for the money they borrow from you, and they lend money at rates of six to nine percent, they are making money with someone else's money. This method has proven successful for centuries in all different parts of the world.

The process of using other people's money to buy life insurance is quite simple. First, you borrow money from a bank. Ideally, you want to borrow money at a favorable, and possibly tax-deductible, rate. You use the loan proceeds to purchase a life insurance policy. Of course, the loan you take out has interest payments (that may or may not be tax deductible). You may pay the interest payments or let them accrue. You also have to eventually pay back the loan principal. With insurance, you have dividends, cash accumulation, and a death benefit. If the cash accumulation (which may be tax deferred or even tax free) in the insurance policy is large enough to pay off the loan, you can use tax-free loans from the policy to pay off the loan. The remaining death benefit in the insurance policy is then yours.

An alternative method, after securing the loan and purchasing the insurance policy, is to use the dividends to pay the interest on the loan. If you borrowed $100,000 to buy a $500,000 life insurance policy and the dividends are large enough to pay the interest payments, you can agree to pay off the $100,000 loan with a portion of the death benefit from the insurance. In this case, your family still has $400,000 left. That's $400,000 that cost you $0 out of pocket. Here's an example to illustrate the point.

Years ago, my firm had a client secure an interest-only home equity loan for around two percent. Many clients take out home equity loans at rates of three to five percent. If you assume a 30 to 50 percent marginal income tax bracket, these clients received tax deductions that reduced their after-tax loan rates to between 1.5 to 4.0 percent. At the same time, a AAA-rated insurance company credited 5.5 percent (tax free) to its universal life policies and more than 10 percent to its equity-indexed universal life policies. The point is that you can ultimately use the accumulated difference between the crediting rate and the loan rate to pay down the loan principal, too. This will leave the entire death benefit to your family.

Charting a Better Path

The biggest misunderstanding about life insurance is that most people don't see it for what it really is. The average person sees life insurance as an expense. The very wealthy family and successful business owner see life insurance as not just an investment – but as a flexible investment.

Life insurance offers more leverage than any other investment tool. A relatively small premium payment can protect a family from a premature death, protect a business in a buy-sell arrangement, accumulate wealth without taxes, or efficiently transfer the wealth from one generation to another. Despite its fantastic leverage, life insurance's most important characteristic is its flexibility. You don't have to decide exactly how you will use it or what you want to use the life insurance for before you buy it. You can add more premium later, gift the policy to a person or entity, sell the policy, save it for the death benefit, use the cash values for lifetime needs, return the money withdrew, or not return it.

The applications of life insurance can range from the traditional buy-sell, estate planning, and income replacement options to more creative applications such as retirement enhancing and premium financed insurance. Later, you will see three extremely powerful applications of insurance when it is partnered with flexible legal structures to improve the value of businesses, significantly reduce unnecessary taxes, and build mega-estates.

Chapter 27
"Epic Win" and a Mini Pet Giraffe

"Wealth is not about having a lot of money;
it's about having a lot of options."

—Chris Rock

In 2010, DirecTV kicked off a multiyear advertising campaign during the coveted Super Bowl ad blitz. The ads featured a Russian billionaire, Gregor, who had a couple of famous lines, "Epic Win" and "Opulence, I has it." The real star of the campaigns was his mini pet giraffe. The premise was that a billionaire could actually afford to breed an adorable little lap giraffe. It was so well received that countless gullible (and smitten) viewers fell for the prank that Sokoblovsky Farms was a real location breeding small giraffes.

You may wonder what the hell this has to do with the seeing paths to elevated wealth. Good question. I have had the pleasure of working with three billionaire families. Though none of them had mini giraffes, they did teach me the biggest ideas are actually very small. Still not convinced that bigger isn't always better? Think back to your journey along the 3rd Path when you saw all the major threats to your long-term wealth? Do you remember the myriad taxes that the federal government has? When the tax man comes looking, would you like to look like a really big giraffe with lots of money in those saddle bags? Or, would you prefer to look a whole lot smaller?

Let's look at the most powerful way billionaire families like Gregor think small to win the big game of wealth.

When Willie Sutton Talks, *You* Should Listen

Pardon the pun, but many of you probably remember the 1970s E.F. Hutton commercials, "When EF Hutton talks, people listen." EF Hutton was once a prestigious stock brokerage firm, founded in 1904. Though it was the second largest brokerage firm in the country for several decades, it essentially collapsed (they would say merged) in the late 1980s. A check kiting scandal was followed up by threats of an indictment from the SEC around its Providence, Rhode Island brokers' role in a money-laundering scheme for the Patriarca crime family. Given that I was in high school in Providence at the time, I remember it all too well. Combine the stock market collapse of 1987 with EF Hutton's brokers not listening to the rule makers, and one of the biggest firms in America goes out of business.

On a much lighter and equally nefarious note, we have Slick Willie Sutton. He was called "Slick" because he robbed multiple banks and escaped from custody numerous times. Despite very little education, Sutton has been quoted for decades. While in custody, a journalist for The American Weekly magazine named Fred Curran interviewed Sutton. When asked why he robbed banks, Sutton replied, "That's where the money is." This was a long setup, to give you the clue that "banks" are where the money is. In this case, it has multiple meanings.

The Friendliest Bank Ever – YOURS!

Willie taught us banks have the money. He created a very attractive loan from his banks. He just took the money and never paid it back. If you don't get caught, those are amazing terms. Since you do not want to go to jail, we want to find you terms that are as close to Willie's as possible without being against the law. Impossible? Not at all.

From finance and accounting, we know that loans are neither income to the recipient nor an expense to the lender. When the interest is paid, it is taxable to the recipient. The loan principal, however, is never taxable. These very simple premises: banking, tax-free loans, and interest are the keys to the most powerful wealth transfer strategy available today.

Ideal Candidates for Generational Banking

- Families who have taxable estates of $10,000,000 or more.
- Families who have some assets that will grow at more than three percent per year.
- Families who want to leave a significant amount to future generations.
- Families who want to reduce unnecessary costs of transferring wealth.
- Families who want to protect inheritances from divorce.

This is a technique that we implement to help families reduce hundreds of millions of dollars of unnecessary liabilities. In case it's not obvious, the scenario is a senior generation with the money and a junior generation – which could be children, grandchildren or great grandchildren (or any combination). The people with the money want to receive it with as little friction as legally possible. Since this strategy has multiple variations and relies on many different technical areas of planning, We will oversimplify it to give you an idea of the power of the planning. If you want more information, you can contact me at www.chrisjarvis.me/contact with Generational Banking in the subject line. I will send you a more comprehensive packet. Here is an example:

Step 1 – "Bank" Invests (or Loans) $25,000,000 with Junior Generation
The senior generation is the bank. It can lend or invest family owned stocks, bonds, real estate, or even shares of family businesses into an entity (LLC) that is owned by the junior generation. Because the bank is "family friendly," the terms of the are as follows:

1. Two percent annual return. This is acceptable since the IRS' long term Applicable Federal Rate (AFR) = 1.15 percent as of 05/2020.
2. Repayment of principal and interest are deferred until the dissolution of the LLC
3. LLC will be dissolved at the time of death of the last remaining child (two children)

WHY? The family does this deal because they believe the family assets will grow at a rate significantly greater than two percent per year. The IRS sets the rate for interfamily loans (AFR). If your outlook for your assets is greater than AFR, you should seriously consider this technique.

Step 2 – Bank Requires LLC to "Secure" Investment
The senior generation will make this investment as long as the LLC purchases a life insurance policy on the two children. The policy will be crafted to have adequate death benefit to repay the senior generation all of its investment plus growth at the time of the children's death. This is almost always done by purchasing life insurance from "A" rated (or higher) life insurance carriers. Though there are assets in the LLC to serve as collateral, the existence of the insurance policy gives the family greater investment flexibility (See Step 3).

Step 3 – LLC Invests and Manages Assets for Long-Term Benefit
The LLC may choose to keep the assets the same, make changes, buy, sell, mortgage or alter the investments that were originally used as the senior generation's contribution to the LLC. The taxes from the investments in the LLC do NOT create a 2nd level of taxation as the LLC is a flow-through entity for tax purposes. The strategy is tax neutral. No more or less income tax is likely to be generated with this technique while the LLC is operating.

How much does this benefit the family?
Usually the life insurance costs approximately 20 percent of the original investment. When this is the case, you have essentially locked in the "Friction" to the estate at 20 percent of the value at the time of the investment. In this case, that would be $5,000,000.

The rest of the family money, $20 million, is invested for the benefit of the junior generations. Let's assume that the assets grew at six percent (after tax) and the money was only invested for 24 years before the children passed away. The $20 million would become $80 million. This would be tax free to the heirs.

Contrast this with NOT doing the planning. If the $25 million of taxable family assets had grown at six percent for 24 years, it would have grown to $100 million. Then, there would have been $40 million of estate taxes, netting $60 million to the heirs.

The Generational Banking concept with insurance collateral created 33 percent more in LLC assets, or $20 million, to the heirs. But wait, there's more!

That life insurance policy didn't just disappear. The death benefit at the end of 24 years is now slightly more than $40,000,000. The LLC received the life insurance proceeds and used them to repay the senior generation (bank) for its original investment plus 24 year of interest. The estate of the senior generation will pay income taxes on the $15 million of interest. Even if you assume a 50 percent income tax bracket, that still leaves $32.5 million dollars.

If those funds are taxed at 40 percent before reaching heirs, that's another $19.5 million bringing the total net of taxes to heirs of $99.5 million. The result is 99.5% of what the family would have invested (before any transfer taxes) ultimately makes it to the junior generations. That means you have an effective 0.5 percent friction on the family wealth. That's a lower percentage tax than you pay on a gallon of gasoline.

Charting a Better Path

Super wealthy families stay super wealthy because they don't throw money away. They are aware of all the ways to build, preserve, and transfer wealth. More importantly, they are aware that every time you move money, there are costs: sales taxes, property taxes, income taxes, gift taxes, etc. By taking advantage of low interest rates and utilizing the powerful leverage of life insurance, they transfer wealth from one generation to another, or from a company to its owners or employers (foreshadow for the powerful TrEE chapter later), at almost no cost.

These are powerful strategies people who are so busy "working" never have time to investigate or implement. These are steps that can make all the difference. If you are interested, please do not hesitate to call me to help you assess the opportunity for your family or your business. mail@chrisjarvis.me or 817-442-6007.

Chapter 28
Let Them Eat Zebra Cake?

Giraffes may be very intelligent, but I doubt they know much about the French Revolution. Marie Antoinette famously said, "let them eat cake!" The starving population was less amused by this than they were at the site of her head rolling from the guillotine. Despite my best efforts to get my teens and tweens to eat relatively healthy, their "cake" of choice happens to be a zebra cake. Think "Twinkie" meets a Ding Dong or a Ho-ho. Never mind.

The confluence of the French Revolution and the box of high fructose corn syrup treats with a 200-year half-life that feel good in the moment, with long-term negative health consequences is our metaphor du jour. Often, business-owner employers don't think before they speak or act – and it comes back to haunt them. You don't want to give your valued employees something that may seem simple and sweet in the beginning, when you know it will ultimately be bad for them. Sure, my kids need to learn right from wrong with their food choices, but I know that a box in the pantry will be gone in less than 24 hours. I am suggesting that you take a longer-term approach to what you offer your employees because you will need their help long term. Here are a few unconventional "giraffe" perspectives for you to consider.

Retirement Plans are for Suckers. Everyone "has to" have a retirement plan. Without one, people wouldn't ever want to work for you. Here are seven reasons why you should rethink your traditional retirement plan.

1. **Employees don't really want it.**
   How do I know this? Consider one of my good friends and clients, Dr. Andy. Dr. Andy has run a very successful medical practice in Central Texas for twenty years. At any given time, he may have 100-120 full time employees. He pays well and offers very generous benefits, including a 401k plan. Over the last twenty years, 200 employees who were previously enrolled in his 401k plan have left his employment. Do you want to guess how many of them have

rolled over their investment accounts to IRAs? One. Not one guess, one person. Of 200 employees, 199 cashed in their 401k right after leaving. None of them were over the age of 59 ½ at the time. This means that all of them, who were in their prime working years, paid full ordinary income taxes, plus a ten percent early withdrawal penalty, to have access to the money immediately.

Here is "the test" to see if your employees really want their 401(k) plan. Don't ask your human resources person for an opinion and don't survey the employees if they want the plan. Every employee would rather have something than not have it. The real test is to ask each employee the following question:

> "Last year, I contributed $1,500 to your 401(k) plan. I am considering a change of plan to give employees a choice. I could continue the plan as it is now or pay you a bonus of $1,200 at the holidays. Which would you choose?"

So far, 100 percent of my friends and clients who surveyed their employees told me, "Nearly every employee chose the cash." If we used the example above as a barometer, we could save 20 percent of our retirement planning dollars AND have a lot more flexibility – which we will explain shortly.

2. **Executives can't utilize retirement plans effectively.**

The maximum contribution for a defined contribution plan in 2020 is $57,000. This number represents 20 percent of the maximum allowable salary of $285,000. This doesn't mean that you can't earn more than $285,000, but all salary above $285,000 is not included for the purposes of calculating allowable contributions. Will this be enough for your most valued employees?

A classmate of mine from business school, Liz Davidson, wrote an article about the history of retirement plans for Workforce.com. Liz estimated that you would need to save 11 times your pre-tax salary before retirement, to support your quality of life after you stop working. If you are making $100,000 per year, it's feasible that you could save $1.1M in a retirement plan. However, if you earn $400,000 per year, it would take outrageous investment returns to turn your $57,000 retirement plan contributions into $4.4M of savings.

3. **Retirement Plans are for Socialists, not for Entrepreneurs**
   In 1974, the Employee Retirement Income Security Act (ERISA) enacted a combination of federal income tax and labor law to establish minimum standards for pension plans in private industry. Over forty years ago, it was very common for an employee to work for an employer for twenty-five to forty years and retire with a pension. The very complicated ERISA rules were designed to protect employees in the short term, which would contribute to long-term economic growth.

   Unfortunately, the result ended up being something less interesting for business owners. Under Employee Retirement Income Security Act of 1974 (ERISA), the retirement plan contributions are based on a percentage of income. A defined benefit plan will factor age into the equation, with older employees generally being able to invest a greater amount. There is no ability to alter the contributions based on performance. These particular plans are not meritocracies. Every forty-three-year-old qualifying employee who earns $50,000 in salary will receive the same retirement plan benefit. Though this may seem fair, it does not help the overly ambitious entrepreneur who wants to reward the best and brightest employees and wants to do so in a way that encourages them to stay with the company long term. Luckily, there are other ways to accomplish this, which we will discuss in the next chapter.
4. **You're a "Muppet" for the Mutual Fund Companies**
   Please indulge me for a little context. In March of 2012, Greg Smith resigned from Goldman Sachs. The former executive director and vice president went out with a bang – penning an Op-Ed page article in the New York Times where he called Goldman's culture "toxic and destructive." Mr. Smith's letter came during the devastating financial crisis. Goldman had emerged as the rich and arrogant perpetrator of the financial wreckage that left many hard-working Americans holding the proverbial bag. Mr. Smith's now-infamous reference was to Muppets — "I have seen five different managing directors refer to their own clients as 'Muppets,' sometimes over internal e-mail."

First, the "Muppet" reference is to Jim Henson's television show. Kermit the Frog, Miss Piggy and Gonzo were just a few of the puppet characters created by Henson. Second, the Goldman Sachs reference has nothing to do with comedy and everything to do with "puppets." My take on Smith's commentary is that Goldman's clients acted as if the firm was pulling the strings. Somehow, when the housing market crashed, investors lost money in their mortgage backed securities and Goldman made billions of dollars. There are very interesting commentaries about this in two documentaries, *The Inside Job* and *The Big Short.* Keep this story in mind as you read about mutual fund companies.

Mutual fund assets held in retirement accounts (IRAs and defined contribution plans including 401(k) plans), stood at $8.0 trillion as of the end of March 2017 (source: Investment Company Institute, ICI.org). That amount represents 47 percent of all mutual fund assets held by retirement plans. $8 trillion dollars! You may ask, why is size a bad thing? I am going to tell you.

You have undoubtedly heard the quote, "It's what you don't know that is going to kill you!" The enormous retirement plan industry has fees that are a secret to most people. Kiplinger quoted an AARP survey where 80 percent of people surveyed had no idea how much they paid in fees for their retirement plans. The lack of transparency is a problem, that Bloomberg tried to tackle in an article dated 8/23/2017. Bloomberg quoted an NEPC investigation of 123 retirement plans. These plans represented $138 billion in total invested assets. The result was that the average expense fee for these plans was 0.41 percent. This is in addition to an average record-keeping fee of $59 per person, per year. Wait! These fees are in addition to the fees for the actual mutual funds themselves.

You can invest in a Vanguard index fund and pay 0.04 percent in fees or, you can invest in the same Vanguard fund inside your retirement plan and pay $59 per year plus 0.44 percent in expenses. I'm too frustrated with the whole industry to dive down a rabbit hole and calculate how much these crazy fees will decimate your retirement. Trust me that the most successful people don't bother with retirement plans in their estate planning.

Phantom Stock, Deferred Compensation & Stock Options are Tax Disasters. Something I have heard many culture consultants and entrepreneurs talk about is, "getting employees to act like owners." One way to do that is to provide every single employee a good amount of stock. You could create an Employee Stock Ownership Plan (ESOP), but that would require you to relinquish a lot of equity, and it may have the same "socialist" vibe we discussed earlier. To create the illusion of ownership, many companies offer phantom stock, deferred compensation or stock options.

The big problem with these options for the employee is tax liability. The owner has all the control of if, when and how the company will be sold. The employees can't really plan for the event, but they get stuck with ordinary income taxes when their phantom stock vests. Deferred compensation is always taxable to the participants. An event that gives the employee "constructive receipt," can trigger a huge tax liability. What about stock options? I have a degree in applied mathematics, am a Certified Financial Planner™ professional and have worked in taxation and business-building for 20 years. I still find the timing and taxation of incentive stock options confusing. And, if you exercise your options, then the stock price drops between your election date and the date you plan to sell the options (one year later hoping for long term capital gains treatment), you can have a tax liability on stock value you never received. It happened frequently in the early 2000s.

Charting a Better Path

You are never going to build wealth working for someone else. You will either invent something amazing or own your own company. Those employees working for you will be the most important people in your wealth creation. The job market is very competitive, and the future job market is going to change considerably. Millennials have very different outlooks on work and their values are not what your parents' values were. You are going to have to meet them where they are — or where they want to be. Offering the same benefits package that you were offered or the same "bennies" as your competitors will not be enough. You must stick your neck out and be the giraffe if you want their help. The next chapter is going to show you exactly how to do that.

Chapter 29
Plant TrEEs *with* and *for* Your Employees

At the beginning of this path, you learned about the very special relationship between the giraffe and the acacia tree. Not only does the tree nourish the giraffe, but it also protects the giraffe by guiding it upwind. As you look even more deeply at the relationship, you see that the acacia tree protects other trees in the area in a way that preserves the food source for future giraffes who wander through the area. Both animal and food source interact in a way that helps each other, and helps other animals, and other trees. This is a relationship unlike any other in the food chain.

The acacia tree and the giraffe have a symbiotic relationship that is truly special. If you are going to beat the odds and reach your ambitious financial goals, you are not going to do it by working harder. You must leverage your time, assets and effort. The only way to do that is to leverage other people. Unless you are an emperor, pharaoh, or king, people around you are not going to dedicate their lives to your success. You will need to create a "win-win" scenario where it's in other people's best interests to help you.

To that point, I constantly preach to my clients, seminar attendees, and Giraffe University members, "The greater number of people who are interested in your success, the greater the probability and level of your success!" There are two proven ways to do this. Along the 6th Path, you will see how to leverage professionals and advisors in a way that will reduce your expenses and improve your results. Now, you are going to pick up your pace and take the master's course in leveraging the people who will have the most immediate impact on your success: your employees.

Leveraging Employees – Master's Course

If you do not own a business, you may find this information very important for some day when you do. If you have no intention of owning a business, you may want to introduce this chapter to your current or future boss — so you can receive a much more attractive long-term compensation package.

Forget what your employment attorney taught you about the definition of "employees." We are not talking about W-2 employees who qualify for benefits. There is no need to disqualify anybody from our potential leverage list as we are trying to increase the number of people who are helping us. To find a better path to success, we want to include anyone who is affiliated with our business in any way whatsoever. Let's expand our definition of employees to include:

Employers Need to Leverage

- Employees & Executives
- Independent Contractors
- Partners (in the case of professionals)
- Investors
- Board of Directors/Advisory Board Members
- Vendors & Suppliers
- Advertisers & Celebrity Endorsers
- Anybody who cashes a check with your name on it!

Don't Fall into the Expense Trap

Your accountant may tell you that all of those people on our list are "below the line" items. Below the line refers to the expenses that fall after your, "top line" revenue number. Historically, you were taught to increase your top line (revenues) and reduce your expenses (items that fall below the line) so you end up with a larger "bottom line" number (which is the top line minus the expenses that fall below the line). The purpose of **giraffeMONEY** is to help you elevate your perspective so you can see a better path to elevated wealth. In this chapter, you will see a creative way to rethink, and restructure how you compensate and motivate these groups of people.

"When people are financially invested, they want a return.
When people are emotionally invested, they want to contribute."

—Simon Sinek

As the business owner, you want to inspire your people to act like owners. You know you can't sustain it with lots of rah-rah. You know you can't afford to just dole out lots of moo-lah. You're looking for that moment of a-ha!

You have to find a way to put your employees in a position where they benefit when you benefit. For the millennial who wants to feel like he is wanted, you must make him understand how he is a vital contributor to your future success. If you can let go of all those other strategies that others want you to use (for their benefit, maybe?), and you can elevate your perspective, you might just see this new, better path to success. We call it TrEE.

The TrEE Program Transforms Expenses into Equity. What kind of expenses? Most successful businesses are inefficiently utilizing valuable capital for incentive compensation, bonuses, employee and executive benefits, deferred compensation, and incentive stock options. While your company may be wasting valuable resources on the aforementioned items, you are also spending valuable time and money on interest payments (if you have debt), compliance reporting and meetings (with lenders), shareholder communications, capital raising (if you need additional capital), shareholder dividends, executive recruiters, new hire training and onboarding, retirement plan onboarding, among others.

How much employee and executive time and company money is spent on all of those areas I just listed? $1,000,000? $10,000,000? $100,000,000? The larger your company, the more you are wasting in those areas. Imagine if you could redeploy the capital in the first list so that your employees could replace much of your need for outside investors, bank financing, and all the unnecessary reporting and aggravation that goes with it. If you didn't have to worry about shareholders and banking covenants, how much more efficient would your people be? How much more profitable would your company be?

If your employees were all participating in the savings and in the excess value creation, would you need to pay a recruiter ever again? Or, would you have the greatest workforce on the planet? Is a 401(k) giving you that kind of return? Are you getting this type of great idea from Fidelity or Deloitte or Northwestern Mutual? Not a chance. I'm not picking on those companies. There isn't a mutual fund company, accounting firm or insurance company coming up with a groundbreaking strategy like TrEE. I know because I have worked with a number of them to help implement plans like this one. They are so in love with their own product lines and their processes that they don't want to hear the truth about what businesses owners need. They just can't handle the truth.

How does TrEE work? When I co-authored the bestselling book, ***Mastering the Art of Success***, with Jack Canfield, I wrote a section called, "Increasing Sales without Ever Selling." One of the strategies I shared was to partner with your clients. TrEE is a partnership in the truest sense. It is a partnership between the company, the employees, and the investors. By eliminating all of those wasted expenses, the company will significantly increase its earnings. The increased earnings will increase the value of the company. How much the company increases its value will depend on the price to earnings ratio, or the multiple (of earnings) that is ultimately paid at sale. Everyone, other than the future buyers, will benefit from higher earnings.

In anticipation of fantastic future growth and increased profitability, the company will invest its profits with its employees. That's right! Instead of getting employees to reinvest their tax-inefficient retirement plan dollars back into the company (like employees at Enron did), the company will take its dollars that are taxed at a potentially lower corporate tax rate and invest them with employees. These investments will be done at arm's length rates per Internal Revenue Code guidance. Right now, those rates are less than three percent. That rate will be locked in for the remainder of the employee's lifetime. The employee gets all of the investment value during his or her lifetime. The company will not receive any piece of the employee's investment until the employee dies.

Employees will be able to direct the investment of the proceeds from the employer into a range of investments that fit the individual employees' risk tolerance. One of the investments is life insurance. This investment may be ten to 30 percent of the total investment from the employee, depending on age and health of the employee. That life insurance will protect the employee's family from any unfortunate premature death. The life insurance will also ensure that the company gets repaid for its investment at the death of the employee.

How is TrEE better than deferred compensation? The TrEE investment from the company into the account for the employee is not taxable to the employee. Deferred compensation is taxed as ordinary income tax rates. TrEE is a separate account, not subject to creditors of the company. Deferred compensation benefits could be seized by a creditor of the company. TrEE give the employees access and control to funds right away. Deferred Compensation is not available to the employee for use or control.

Deferred compensation is a liability to the company. When it is paid, it is an expense to the company, lowering its earnings. TrEE is an asset to the company. It improves the value of the company and will enhance the value at the time of sale.

In our experience, incentive compensation, stock options and bonuses that get restructured as TrEE benefits create a fifty to seventy five percent increase in after tax benefits to the employees. That value is in addition to the significant benefit that TrEE affords the sponsoring company. If a company redeploys $10,000,000 of bonuses or incentive compensation in a given year, and that company has a Price to Earnings (P/E) ratio of fifteen, the company's total value will increase by $150,000,000 for the shareholders. If your company is in a lower growth industry and you someday sell for a multiple of six times earnings, the owners will get $60,000,000 more for the sale of the company. Where else can you do something great for your employees AND create massive value for the owners at the same time?

Who is the best candidate for TrEE? TrEE can be altered to fit the specific needs of the sponsoring company. It works particularly well for:

- Not-for-profit institutions
- Universities (for presidents, coaches, highly paid staff)
- Companies with retained earnings
- Companies with net operating losses (NOLs)
- Companies with loss carry forwards
- Companies with large amounts of depreciable equipment
- Organizations where excessive compensation is bad publicity
- Healthcare companies that pay physicians (directly or indirectly)
- Private equity owned portfolio companies
- Family businesses that want to transfer to future generations
- Companies with highly paid boards of directors
- Companies that want to sell in the next three years
- Publicly traded companies with high P/E ratios
- Companies that have below expected earnings
- Turnaround and leveraged buyout (LBO) situations
- CPA firms with unfunded defined benefit plans
- Law firms with unfunded defined benefit plans

- Companies that pays celebrity or athletes endorsers
- Entertainment industry (film, television, professional sports)
- Any firm that pays "talent" millions of dollars per year
- Any company that pays royalties (television, music, etc.)

Charting a Better Path

The problem with most "tried and true" and common-sense solutions is that they have been simplified and streamlined for maximum applicability. Though this process reduces the costs of implementation, the solutions we are left with are neither easily customized, nor particularly applicable for higher earning giraffes.

TrEE is a very flexible structure that works well in various circumstances. Though the design of the plan will vary significantly from one client to the next, TrEE can be used to help a startup improve its profitability, help a nonprofit avoid unnecessary excise taxes on key employees, help a private equity firm increase the value of a portfolio company it plans to sell, and even help a public company improve the value of its stock by tens or hundreds of millions of dollars.

One application of the program has been favorably reviewed by the head of global tax at one of the Big Four accounting firms. If you are interested in seeing how TrEE might work for you or for one of your clients. These are the most fun projects we handle, so this is one of only two shameless plugs I will put in the book. You can find us www.ChrisJarvis.me/contact or call me at 817-442-6007.

6th PATH
Stretch Your Advisors — for Your Benefit

"Whoever pays the consultant gets pretty much what they want to hear."
—Matthew Stewart

It's a jungle out there—actually its usually a Savannah for the giraffe, but you get the metaphor.

When you follow the herd, you are surrounded by a large group looking for the same things. There is little need, or room, to improvise. Life is pretty simple — until you decided that you want more. That changes when you decide to leave the herds who are not ready (or willing) to change to reach elevated levels of wealth. They look at you differently and treat you differently, too.

I know the feeling. I have been there three times! When I left my actuarial career to go school to get an MBA, people couldn't believe that I would give up such a good job, borrow money, and go back to school full-time. When I sold my home on the beach in Southern California, people couldn't fathom how I could trade California beaches for the pick-up trucks and gun racks of Texas. When I sold my company in 2016, people couldn't believe that I would leave an industry where I had experienced so much success for 25 years. In all these cases, my decisions were the right ones – for me.

On this journey, you will abandon familiar surroundings and encounter unfamiliar challenges. The complications of your plans, and your growing wealth, will require different expertise and greater coordination. The people you looked to for advice for years, or even decades, may no longer be as valuable to you. When you realize that you have outgrown your advisors (or soon will), you may feel alone – like the giraffe in the desert.

On this path, you will more clearly see how professionals and advisory firms are structured, where the inherent conflicts of interest exist, and most importantly how to change the relationships to create a more productive dynamic.

I have had the pleasure of teaching or coaching thousands of advisors in the fields of finance, investing, insurance, accounting and law. I have built professional alliances and developed strong relationships with hundreds of advisors over the past three decades. Some of them are proud supporters of www.GiraffeUniversity.com. If you want an introduction to someone who can help you, please feel free to reach out to me at www.chrisjarvis.me/contact.

Chapter 30
Even Giraffes Stop and Ask for Directions

"You will appear to be 'off-course' for most of your journey.
Keep moving and look for people to guide you."
—Jack Canfield, *The Success Principles*

Standing 20 feet above the plains, the giraffe boasts the most elevated perspective of any land mammal. This allows the giraffe to see paths others can't — and ultimately reach places most won't. Despite this extraordinary vision, giraffes are still limited in what they can see. They cannot see what's behind them, what's beyond the horizon, and what's hiding along the path. To be better prepared for the road ahead, giraffes would love to ask the advice of another who has already been where they are heading.

Before you broke free from the herd, you may have asked:

- How can I make more money?
- Why do I need to start, or restructure, my business?
- Where should I invest?
- What structures and insurances do I need to protect myself?
- When do I make my next move?
- Who is going to help me do all this?

You probably found answers for many of these questions. If you have enjoyed some financial success, you may have confidence in your ability to navigate this space alone. This can be a dangerous mindset that will limit your growth. As you attain more wealth, things become more complicated. You start asking more complicated questions:

- Where can I find cheaper money to fuel my growth?
- How, when, and at what price will I sell my company?
- How do I legally eliminate these huge tax bills?
- When is it time to own my own bank or insurance company?
- How do I protect my kids' inheritance from divorce without suggesting something that will make them hate me?
- Will anyone give me good advice that isn't self-serving?

It shouldn't come as a surprise that with greater success comes greater complexity, both professionally and personally. You could undoubtedly research the answers to each of these questions, but you won't do that. Why? You already understand that your time is your most valuable asset. With leverage as the key to long-term wealth generation, you recall from the 2nd Path that leveraging other people is the most powerful form because it's the only way for you to get more than 24 hours of work done in a day.

As your make your way down the path toward elevated wealth, you will have an opportunity to create leverage through multiple advisors. You can expect to interact with dozens of professionals and hundreds of supporting staff at their firms. They can help you navigate accounting, business planning, insurance, investing, retirement, risk management, taxes, estate planning and countless subspecialties within each field.

When utilized properly, advisors can help you supercharge the speed of your journey along the path in four ways. First, they will save you time and give you the answers you need right away. Second, they will oversee, implement and manage time-consuming and tedious processes. Third, they will help you identify potential pitfalls before they arise so you can steer clear of them. Fourth, as a result of the time and aggravation they will save you in the first three areas, advisors will free you up to spend time doing the things that excite you and that make money.

Which Way to My Seat?

After completing an MBA at the Anderson School (at UCLA), I stayed in Southern California. During my ten years there, it was abundantly clear that Los Angeles was a "Showbiz" town. In the same way finance dominates conversation in New York City, and politics is the favorite sport in Washington DC, the entertainment industry ruled the City of Angels. The biggest events for the entire year were the Academy Awards (or Oscars) and the Screen Actors Guild (SAG) Awards.

For the lucky insiders, there were invites to big parties. For Average Joe's, there were Oscar watch parties that were much more elaborate than those for the Super Bowl. For people who want to merge the two worlds, they would actually GO to the Oscars or SAG Awards. How? As seat fillers, of course. You never see a shot of the crowd with empty seats. That's because volunteer seat fillers will step in and take the seat of a celebrity who has to step out to use the bathroom, prepare to read a nomination or winner, or have a slight nervous breakdown after not winning.

As a side note, the actor Geoffrey Rush won the Oscar and SAG Awards for Outstanding Performance by Male Actor in a Leading Role ("Best Actor") for his portrayal of David Helfgott in the movie *Shine* in 1996. My good friend Dave Schwartz happened to be sitting at the table with Rush and the cast of *Shine*. Everyone at the table, including Dave (who had never met Geoffrey Rush) jumped up and celebrated. All the congratulating looked normal and was a great event for Dave, but I digress.

Why do I share this? Allow me to mix metaphors for a moment. Being on the team or having a seat on the bus doesn't make you valuable. Dave Schwartz happened to be sitting at the table when the award was announced, but he did not get to go up on stage and he certainly does not have an Oscar on his mantle at home.

Your advisory team may be almost as important to you and your family as your executive and management teams are to your business. By taking a more structured and scientific approach to building this team correctly from the start, you will likely save yourself valuable time, preserve a valuable friendship or two, and reach your goals faster, with fewer headaches. Once you have your group of core advisors from multiple disciplines, it's time to help them to help you (queue Tom Cruise and Cuba Gooding Jr. in *Jerry McGuire*).

Charting a Better Path

You can't expect to achieve affluence while maintaining your sanity unless you build the right team of advisors. Trying to achieve financial success without a team of advisors is like trying to get 100 percent of your healthcare from one doctor. Without the help of orthopedists, dermatologists, neurologists, obstetricians, and dozens of other specialists, your health would certainly suffer. Society has benefited from the developing expertise in different areas of medicine. The giraffe earners and giraffe builders have benefited from leveraging expertise from many different financial planning areas. You can, too.

As you continue down this path, you will see that the process of building and maintaining wealth faces challenges from all areas of law, accounting, finance, insurance, and business. Once you accept this reality, you will start to embrace the need to leverage the expertise of advisors in multiple areas. Most importantly, you will see that monitoring, coordinating, and managing so many advisors will become a full-time job – and will take you away from the "giraffe-like" things that made you your money in the first place.

What types of advisors do the affluent utilize? How do you divide the responsibilities within the team? How do you choose the actual advisors? We will answer all of those questions and identify potential conflicts of interest in working with each type of advisor. Lastly, in this path, we will point out some of the ways you can re-engineer the working relationships with different classes of advisors to make sure they are working for you.

Chapter 31
Sun Tzu is Chinese for "Giraffe"

"If you do not seek out allies and helpers,
then you will be isolated and weak."
—Sun Tzu, *The Art of War*

In the last chapter, you may have noticed a subtle reference to Jim Collin's bestselling book, ***Good to Great.*** Collins refers to "getting the right people on the bus" as a mantra for attracting people with the proper attitude for your management team. This is true for your personal wealth and of the utmost importance for any business you start, manage or own.

Before you can choose those advisors, delegate responsibilities, or begin to benefit from the leverage they will offer, you should review the most common advisors who assist families with growing, preserving and transferring wealth. To make this chapter more valuable, we want to go beyond a review of basic skills and functions. You will see some of the mistakes people make when working with each type of advisor so you can get more out of your relationships. In the next chapter, we will review some very creative alternatives to the typical relationships most clients have with these advisors:

- Accountants
- Attorneys
- Insurance agents & brokers
- Investment advisors
- Financial planners

When you complete this chapter, you will know how to avoid the biggest pitfalls in working with each class of advisors. In the next two chapters, you will learn how to better build and manage teams, and how to create win-win relationships. These will help you increase the impact of your advisors while either saving or making money in the process.

Accountants

The term accountant will be used to generically describe an accountant, certified public accountant (CPA) or enrolled agent (EA). What they do: Accountants are trained and licensed to prepare tax returns for submission to the Internal Revenue Service. Each state has its own licensing and accreditation procedures for accountants and CPAs. In the most desirable client-advisor relationship, the accountants also provide clients with advice on tax matters. Accountants generally bill by the hour.

Potential Conflict: Bigger Not Always Better

In 2016, I had a meeting with the private client group of a Big Four firm. They told me that their group was forbidden from discussing advanced strategies with its CEO and high net worth clients. The reason they gave me was that the powers that be in the organization didn't want an overzealous IRS agent to attack the firm for its "aggressive tax planning." The bad press could threaten the firm's very profitable audit practice. They suggested that a better outcome would be for their high-income executives to hire me for planning and return to the Big Four firm for the accounting and compliance needs associated with the strategies. It may sound totally absurd, but it is 100 percent true.

Attorneys

The term *attorney* describes someone admitted to the Bar Association in the state(s) in which he or she practices. Attorneys may specialize in corporate issues, litigation, labor law, income tax, estate planning or dozens of other specialties. You undoubtedly have a number of them working for you. They generally charge by the hour, but some flat fee work is possible.

Potential Conflict: To Fee or Not to Fee.

The attorney situation is similar to the accounting conflict. There are so many different specialties that one attorney, or even one firm, may struggle to help you in all areas of need. I have been in two major litigations in my career. In each case, the lawyers earned hundreds of thousands of dollars and the cases extended over multiple years. In the end, I won more money than the attorneys were paid. You could say that the attorneys provided a valuable service by winning me money. But that conclusion does not take into consideration the pain, suffering, and worry I endured with years of litigation. I am not saying that I wouldn't do it all over again, but I would seriously consider it.

Since there is very little recurring revenue for attorneys from clients, new engagements must be generated annually. This may create an incentive for attorneys to either extend the work or to refer you to their colleagues.

Insurance Agents and Brokers

Insurance agents and *brokers* provide various types of insurance policies to clients. Some insurance professionals also offer financial planning or investment solutions. Insurance agents and brokers must have a resident agent license in the state in which they reside. CERTIFIED FINANCIAL PLANNER™ professionals, accountants, investment advisors, and attorneys can all secure life insurance licenses.

Potential Conflict: They Don't Work for You.

Follow the money. You pay the insurance company a premium for your insurance product. The insurance companies pay the insurance agents' commissions on their sales. You don't generally pay the insurance agent anything. Some agents are restricted or heavily motivated to sell the products of one company (Northwestern Mutual, New York Life, Mass Mutual, etc.) because they have a subsidized career agent contract. Other independent agents have the freedom to sell any company, but almost every agent is part of some affinity group or organization that offers additional support, awards or other incentives to sell their products.

Though it is not required by law (as yet) for agents to disclose commissions, I highly suggest that you ask your agent or broker to tell you exactly what he or she makes in hard (direct) and soft (indirect) payments for selling you the policy. If you are afraid to tell your client how you get paid and how much you get paid for the service you are providing, then maybe there is something wrong with this relationship. Insurance plays a huge role in the planning for most of my clients. It's a shame that the shady sales practices and less morally directed salespeople give the industry a bad name. Note: Before you accuse me of bashing the industry, you should know that I have been one of the top insurance agents in the country for the better part of fifteen years and have won top agent honors (out of 14,000 licensed to work with them) for one particular company three separate times, as well as sales awards with three other companies. This is because I create partnerships with my clients. (There is a great idea for lowering your commission costs in the next chapter).

Investment Advisors

We use the term *investment advisor* to include money managers, stockbrokers, private client service groups, private bankers, private wealth advisors and we might even be able to throw private equity firms into this "private" group. These advisors have to study and pass a three-hour securities exam and a ninety-minute ethics exam, or file as an independent registered investment advisor directly with the U.S. Securities and Exchange Commission. Investment advisors handle investments for clients. They typically take a fee based on the amount of assets they manage. Some have incentive-based compensation as well. In my experience, few consider taxes.

Limitation

Most focus on gross, pre-tax returns and fail to adequately manage taxes. The majority of investments may belong to pensions, endowments or other corporate accounts – which are less sensitive to taxation than the personal holdings of the most successful families.

Potential Conflict: It's always a good time to buy.

Investment advisors are paid based on the assets under management (AUM). The more money they are investing for their clients, the more money they earn for the firm and for themselves. Many of my colleagues and I joke that there are only two stories you get from your investment guy:

1) The market is up. You want to stay in the market
2) The market is down. It's a great time to buy!

It's absolutely amazing. The guys who get paid to manage money always think it's a good time for you to put more money in the market and its never a good time to sell and take your money out of the market altogether.

Financial Planner

We use the term *financial planner* to describe someone who charges a fee to create a financial plan for a client. Sometimes, this is a certified financial planner who has taken six courses over a number of years, met an ethics standard, and passed a much more rigorous exam than the other financial and insurance professionals. I have passed them all, and the CFP is by far the hardest. The biggest difference between the CERTIFIED FINANCIAL PLANNER™ professional and other insurance-related advisors is that the CFP® has a fiduciary relationship. This means he or she has to put your interests ahead of his. An insurance agent only has to meet a suitability standard. As long as he isn't hurting you, it is ok if the planning is better for him, than for you. Someone with a CFP designation could not do that while complying with the organization's Code of Ethics.

Potential Conflicts: Wolf in Sheep's Clothing?
The financial planner can be a salesperson in disguise. It can be hard to distinguish between the true planner and the disguised salesperson, focused on ultimately selling insurance products or investment management services. You may have to ask a few questions to find out what the real motivations are for the planner. You may also, when hiring the planner, suggest that you want a 100 percent unbiased person to do the planning and that you may use someone else for the products. Suggest he/she quote you a fee assuming that you would not use them for any implementation. It may help you figure out the motivations if they are still unclear.

You now know a little more about each discipline that may be represented on your team. Before you learn to create more efficient working relationships with them, you need to make sure you have the right team.

Mercenaries-for-Hire Have a Place

Sticking with the *Art of War* theme, we should consider the role of mercenaries-for-hire. Historically, they were not part of an army, but they were paid to come in, do a job, and leave. In addition to the list of advisors described in this chapter, you will need the help of other professionals such as:

- Business or corporate attorneys
- Investment bankers (to help you prepare and sell your company)
- Private equity investors or private bankers
- Real estate attorneys & brokers
- Retirement specialists
- And others.

Each of these experts may have a specific role to play in the teamwork required for your long-term planning. The list above may be very important at certain times, but they are unlikely to be involved for long periods of time.

Charting a Better Path

You will be making money, so you need the help of accountants who can help you remain compliant. Hopefully, you find creative CPAs who can pay for themselves by showing you how to legally reduce your tax burden. Hopefully your attorneys will not only create great documents for your family and your business, but they will also be open minded to new strategies that will help you grow your wealth. Your financial, insurance and investment advisors will help you access products. The goal is to find one who understands taxes and legal structures and can serve as an invaluable quarterback on your team.

You can see how different types of professionals add value to your advisory team. You may even foresee how you and your family can reap additional benefits by having work together to handle complicated challenges. Before you jump into hiring team members, it is important to learn from the mistakes of thousands of people before you. Read the next chapter on the seven mistakes to avoid when building and working with your team. This could save you a lot of time, money, and aggravation in the long run.

Chapter 32
You Can Still Trip Along the Easy Path

"Never underestimate the power of stupid people in large groups."
—George Carlin

When a giraffe makes a big mistake, it can end in death. Luckily, the deadly sins of wealth will only cost you time and money — and perhaps some embarrassment. Over decades working with wealthy clients, I have seen many recurring mistakes when it comes to selecting and working with professionals. Though these "sins" are common, they and the costly penance they bring can both be avoided.

gira*ffe*MONEY Red Flags

- You have had the same group of advisors for many years.
- You don't interview potential replacement advisors.
- Your advisors don't bring new recommendations regularly.
- Your advisors reject ideas with no detailed explanations.
- Your advisors are too familiar, and don't challenge each other.
- You rarely, if ever, pay for second opinions.
- Your advisory team does not meet regularly to coordinate.
- You feel guilty replacing one of your advisors.

Do any of these warning signs hit too close to home? If so, you may need to consider restructuring your advisory board, adding new blood on your advisory team, or changing the dynamics and expectations of the advisors who work with you, your family and your company.

Let's review of a couple of the biggest mistakes people make when trying to leverage advisors.

Pitfall No. 1: Friends or Family as Advisors

One of the biggest mistakes we see is the inclusion of friends and family on the planning team. We can't fault people for thinking that trust is important when choosing people to help manage wealth. Trust is of the utmost importance. However, unless you are willing to lose the friendship to achieve the financial goals, you should avoid this situation.

It is perfectly acceptable to become friendly with your advisors. This is appropriate because the friendship will have grown out of a business relationship. However, when the relationship begins as a friendship, problems may arise when you disagree on a course of action or when the advisor makes a mistake. It's not personal, it's business. Treat it accordingly.

Pitfall No. 2: Choosing Only Local Team Members

Choose the best possible team, irrespective of geographic location. The best available team members need not be the best available advisors in your zip code, city, or county. I am on the advisory board of the University of South Carolina School of Medicine and I fly to family board meetings all over the country. Modern technology facilitates collaboration, no matter where the experts on your team are located. Unlike the surgeon who needs to be in the room to perform surgery, a financial or legal professional doesn't need to be in the room to do what he or she does well. Don't be afraid to enlist the best advisors you can find—even if they are not in your backyard. The cost of a few airline tickets may be a small price to pay for outstanding advice.

Pitfall No. 3: If It Ain't Broke, Don't Fix It

Nearly every financial plan can be improved. Working with someone for 10 or 20 years is not a reason to continue with the same advisor. If you applied that logic to medicine, adult patients would still be seeing their pediatricians. There is a high likelihood that, as you accumulate wealth, your financial needs will change, and you will require advisors who possess greater capabilities and expertise.

It is imperative to continually re-evaluate your team and objectively review if they are competent to handle your current financial challenges. When we ask clients why they stuck with advisors whose expertise they had outgrown, the justification is rarely concrete. We get answers such as "We've been together so long, I'd hate to change now," or "If it ain't broke, don't fix it." This begs the question: "How do you know 'it ain't broke' if you don't get a second opinion?" Consider this case study:

Case Study: Nick the Neurosurgeon

Nick, a neurosurgeon in Florida, contacted my firm after reading one of our books. While his income was more than $1 million per year and he was part of a very successful practice, he still used the same local lawyer who created his wills 20 years earlier. When we were in Florida, we had a meeting with this attorney. We found it was troubling, but not uncommon: He was providing suboptimal service to Nick without knowing it.

Though he was able to handle many elements of Nick's planning, he had little experience and understanding of the advanced techniques that could be used by a doctor earning more than $1 million per year. While this gentleman may have been an acceptable choice for the doctor when he was starting out, continuing to use this attorney as his primary advisor was a mistake for Nick. To avoid this situation, we recommend that you periodically interview new advisors as your needs change.

Pitfall No. 4: Never Getting a Second Opinion

A good way to grade your existing advisors and test the competencies of potential team members is to get a second opinion on your financial plan. Seek out well-respected advisors, expect to pay them for their analysis, and be open to their opinions. Your planning team should consist of talented advisors who want your business—but don't need your business. Stepping through this short-term engagement exercise will provide insight into how organized their firm is and how well they communicate. You are auditioning them for a very important position on your personal board of directors. Treat the process that way.

Of the flaws discussed here, not getting a second opinion is the most damaging. Unfortunately, it is also the most common. It is most damaging because a second opinion is the primary way of identifying planning mistakes or noticeable omissions from your planning. Just as good physicians encourage patients to get a second opinion, good advisors should encourage their clients to do the same.

Case Study: The Value of a Second Opinion

An attorney friend in New York was retained to perform an audit for a long-term client. The client, a successful businessman, was concerned that he might become an IRS target. He hired the firm to perform an audit of his personal and various business income tax returns for the previous five years. What the firm found was shocking. Even though

> this client had used four different accounting firms for his various returns (including a well-known firm with 500-plus employees), the taxes he had paid were far from what he owed. Luckily for him, it was an overpayment of more than $3 million.

This is a true story. Because of the self-imposed audit that the firm oversaw, the client was able to file amended tax returns and receive a huge refund from the IRS and state tax agency. Luckily for him, he was concerned about poor tax advice and spent the money to hire the firm to perform the audit.

Self-test: Have you ever paid an outside advisor to review the work of your attorney, CPA or investment advisor? If not, it is clearly worth a try.

Pitfall No. 5: Letting People Kiss Your Ass

Previously, I wrote a book that warned people not to "Hire Sycophants." I must have had a bunch of them around me to let such a pompous title go through. I have never used that word conversationally, but at least I can admit now what an ass I was when I wrote that. When I survey successful clients for advice they would offer to others, I received many suggestions, including: "find experts," "don't look for 'yes men,'" and "hire people smarter than you."

I put all of these in the same category because the end result is the same. Wealth is generated from proficiency or expertise. The most successful clients realize they needed to focus on what they do very well. They understand they can't be experts at everything, so they leverage other people's expertise while they spend most of their time doing what makes the most money. To successfully implement this strategy, they hire people who know things they don't know and who are willing to disagree with them. Good advisors don't believe the customer is always right.

My most successful clients have told me that they have enough sycophancy in their lives. Interestingly, these successful, influential people cherish the moments when advisors stand up to challenge a position or question a decision. The client sees this as an opportunity to improve his or her position. Some enjoy the challenge.

Pitfall No. 6: Ignoring Need for Outside Expertise

If your medical condition necessitated a stent, you would not go to a general practitioner for this procedure. You probably wouldn't be happy just seeing any cardiologist. You would probably seek the help of an interventional cardiologist to handle this procedure. The point is that medicine is highly specialized. If you have a specific issue, you want a physician properly trained and experienced with this particular issue.

Advanced financial planning is similarly complex. Let's look at the ever-changing U.S. tax law to illustrate this. The lengthy and confusing Internal Revenue Code is a picture of complexity. IRS revenue rulings, private letter rulings, tax memoranda, announcements, circulars, tax court, and Federal court cases only serve to add complexity to the field. In any law library, you are likely to see an entire floor dedicated to tax documentation.

No single person can be an expert in all areas of tax law. The taxation issues that require guidance typically include retirement planning, income structuring (salary vs. bonus), payroll tax, corporate structure choices (S corp or C corp?), whether to implement a deferred compensation plan, estate-tax planning, taxation on sales of real estate, individual tax returns, corporate tax returns, and the complicated tax rules that surround buying or selling a medical practice. All of these areas are tax sub-specialties that require a subspecialist's knowledge.

Self-test: Ask your CPA or attorney which tax areas noted above are within his or her expertise. Ask the advisor how they would handle an issue for you that occurred outside of this area.

Pitfall No. 7: Failing to Insist on Advisor Coordination

Even if you have a team of highly experienced advisors in the fields of tax, law, insurance, and investments, your plan can still be in disarray. If the advisors are not collaborating to optimize the application of their collective expertise to implement a comprehensive, multi-disciplinary plan for your benefit, your planning will suffer.

There are many common symptoms of a disjointed plan. For example, clients who come to our offices have paid a technically sound attorney to create a comprehensive living trust, but the family's assets have not yet been titled to the trust (potentially making the document useless).

I frequently see life insurance policies and life insurance trusts that, because the proper steps were not taken to combine the two vehicles, do not work as they should. As a result, the death benefit of the insurance may be unnecessarily taxed at rates as high as 50 percent. I notice investment accounts that are managed as if they are part of a pension, with no regard for taxation—and the end result is often a 24 to 45 percent reduction in the gain of the investments.

Conflicting advice from professionals in different areas, or a lack of respect for the opinions of other professionals, often leads to planning inertia or just plain bad planning. Like the radiologist, surgeon, and anesthesiologist who must work together to make sure a patient has a successful surgery, your CPA, attorney and financial advisors must work together in order to help you successfully achieve your financial goals. If the surgeon never saw the films or charts, or the anesthesiologist and surgeon didn't speak with one another, the likelihood of an optimal outcome would be reduced.

Self-test: Have your CPA, attorney, financial, and insurance advisors met to discuss and coordinate your planning at least once in the past 12 months? If not, there is a significant chance that your planning is not being well coordinated.

Charting a Better Path

You can now see that just having advisors is not enough. You need a team of people who can appreciate what you are trying to accomplish and are willing to speak up and challenge you and your other advisors if they don't agree with how something is being done. This is not a book club. The purpose of bringing them together is not so they can become friends. The purpose is to coordinate to help you find better paths to your vision of elevated wealth. If you don't get the right people on the team and set the right conditions, it will greatly affect you.

Once you have a smooth-running team that has healthy arguments, that is just the beginning. You always want to be challenging your team, interviewing for new members, and replacing people as necessary. A healthy advisory team doesn't look like a game of musical chairs, but it does have regular turnover. This strategy not only invites new ideas into your planning, but also helps eliminate the potential for unethical or immoral activities that seem to take place when groups are very familiar with one another.

If you are unsure about the effectiveness or capabilities of your team, want to build a better set of rules for your team, or you want to create a team of advisors, please feel free to contact me (www.chrisJarvis.me). I have helped many families and privately held businesses interview, hire and create very effective teams. It will be a good use of your time and money to leverage me and my people to help you build your support team.

Chapter 33
When Your Pet Tiger Bites You, It's *Your* Fault

"Two things are infinite: the universe and human stupidity; and I'm not sure about the universe."

—Albert Einstein

"In politics, stupidity is not a handicap."

—Napoleon Bonaparte

Are you amazed when you see a news story about some fool who was mauled by an exotic pet, like a tiger? Of course not! Most sane people realize that no matter if you think you have found a way to circumvent Mother Nature, animals will ultimately behave like animals. Given the theme of this Path, you may be wondering if I am suggesting that all advisors are animals. Keep reading and you can decide for yourself.

I grew up in Providence, Rhode Island. The native accent is not nearly as thick as ones from New York or Boston, but it can be strong. I seldom let mine out, but a couple bad night's sleep or more than a couple of cocktails can unleash the accent without warning. When you are giving a speech or running a workshop west of the Mississippi or south of the Mason-Dixon, that slip of the tongue can be startling to a group that assumes I'm a Texan. The similarity between the bite of the tiger and the bear of an accent is that stress often brings us back to who we really are.

Jack Welch, legendary CEO of General Electric, famously took all potential executive hires out for a round of golf. He wanted to see how a person handled adversity before he extended an offer. "It's hard to hide your character when you play golf."

This is not only the same of personality traits, it is also the same with training. I suggest that we will all get busy and face challenges. When that happens, our advisory board members will do what they are trained to do. Attorneys will identify risks. Accountants will organize. Salespeople will sell. Managers with manage. Leaders will lead.

Like zookeepers, you must set the proper boundaries to avoid catastrophes. When it comes to your advisors, it is your responsibility to set the rules of engagement and create procedures that benefit and protect you. The same way people want to see animals in an almost natural habitat, while being completely safe, you want to see your professionals display their unique combination of personality, skills and experience without any risk of them damaging your financial situation. Armed with a greater awareness of the threats in working with different kinds of advisors, you are ready to see practical steps you can take to wrangle your advisors into performing better for you.

Is this Shangri-legal?

Imagine a world where all of your advisors are looking for ways to help you to increase your income, reduce your expenses, and take frustrating things off your plate. Imagine the advisors are working together to accomplish your goals, not operating independently for their own financial gain. Imagine that, instead of seeing invoice after painful invoice from your advisors, you actually make money from this group while getting valuable advice and achieving additional leverage. This may sound like Shangri-La, but it doesn't have to be your Lost Horizon. Here are three things you can do to significantly improve your love-hate relationships with gifted, but expensive professionals.

Annual Retreats.

Whether you are running a wealthy family or a privately held business, you have a complicated situation. People are not only judging you based on performance. The small group around you is also very interested in having a fulfilling relationship with you. It is very difficult to have to make tough decisions for the best interests of the people around you AND maintain a strong emotional connection with all of them at the same time. For example, imagine having to fire your incompetent nephew or a long-time employee who was stealing from you. Even if it's obviously the right thing to do, you may still upset your sister or the rest of the staff who worked with that employee for the last ten years.

The most successful entrepreneurs and family offices arrange semiannual or annual, all-day (or multiple day) meetings with all of their advisors. These can include all family members, all managers and key employees, or all employees (in the case of companies with fewer then 20 people). Sometimes, the costs of flying in advisors to participate in these meetings and paying them their hourly wages could total $50,000-$100,000 per year.

According to Doug Hostetler (of Hostetler Church in Maryland), my favorite family wealth counselor in the world: "Families that make this effort to introduce everyone to the experts on their team during their lifetimes are much more successful at transferring wealth and family values to the next generation. When this happens, family businesses have a much greater chance of beating the odds and surviving to the 2nd, 3rd and 4th generations."

When working with any business that is stagnant or facing severe challenges, the retreat is invaluable. Having led many of these retreats, I see that the employees are far more supportive of, and even excited with, the prospect of changing when they see that they were part of the process in charting the new path. Though many executives believe that employees don't respond well to change, my experience is that the employees are far less connected to the current business model than the people at the top. When someone other than their boss is leading the meeting, they are much more creative and more willing to make important suggestions. Scheduling regular retreats may be the single most valuable thing you do in your company or with your family to get the most value out of the people you are leading.

The Family Office Concept.

Simply put, a family office is a legal entity created for the purpose of treating the family's wealth as a business. Some advisors recommend participating in a multi-family office (serving a number of families) when wealth exceeds $50 million. Single-family offices are advised at either the $100 million or $250 million threshold. A wealth management focused family office may perform centralized management or oversight of investments, tax planning, estate planning, and philanthropic planning. A more comprehensive family office may provide tax compliance work, secure access to private banking and private trust services, manage documents and recordkeeping, handle expenses and bill paying, keep the books, educate family members on finance, provide family support services, and offer family governance.

The most significant difference between a formal family office and an informal set of advisors who work for a wealthy family is in compensation. In the formal family office arrangement, the advisors actually work for the family. This will often include accountants, attorneys, investment advisors and financial planners. The professional employees receive a salary and possibly a bonus or "carry" on certain investments or projects. There are usually no billable hours or commissions. This allows the family to accomplish three things:

1) Ensure advisors are giving the family undivided attention.
2) Align interests and eliminate potential conflicts.
3) Manage, or smooth out, expenses by eliminated large invoices.

You may not wish to go "all in" on the family office for your family, but you may want to borrow some of the pieces of the model. You could buy a block of time from your accountant, attorney and investment advisor with the expressed intent that you are going to get them to work for you during that time and that anything they do doing that time will not be subject to additional billing. By pre-purchasing a certain number of hours, you may get a better rate than if you were subject to hour-by-hour billing. You may also structure the payment to the professionals as "Board of Director" compensation. Your advisors' firms may be more flexible with a Board of Directors arrangement than with reduced billable hours. Each situation will be different.

Self-insured Family.

Historically, insurance brokerage is not included in the family office. I am trying to change that as our firm is implementing insurance brokerage arrangements for a number of our most successful families. By creating a joint venture with an independent insurance agent or agency, you can eliminate that major conflict of interest with the commission-based insurance agent. By owning a company together, you create full transparency of the revenues.

Most interesting to our clients who consider this model, is that the creation of a partnership creates a fiduciary duty between our clients and our firm. Usually, insurance agents are held to a suitability standard (which is a much lower level of care). By creating a legal, fiduciary relationship between us and our clients, we eliminate the fear that the insurance agent or broker is going to do something that is in his best interest, and at the expense of the client. I am proud to say that this is one of my favorite "giraffe" strategies. While everyone else is trying to fight commission disclosure legislation to protect the "secrecy" of commissions, we are creating ways of making the insurance process fully transparent. While everyone fears how the insurance agent might be screwing them, we are creating an arrangement where we have higher standard of care to our clients and we share the revenues with them. We give more and get paid less. Who doesn't like the idea of better service and lower costs?

Charting a Better Path

For the same reason people blame the owner when its exotic pet mauls him, I am going to blame you when you get boring, expensive advice from your advisors. If left to their own devices, attorneys will bill by the hour and give you what previous clients paid them to create. Accountants will often default to the "I don't want to get audited" position — which my colleagues and I refer to as "the maximum tax payment" solution. Investment and insurance professionals usually get paid a commission or fee — and these payments vary by product. Human nature is to lean toward products that offer higher payments.

There is nothing wrong with an attorney giving you a solution that has already worked, an accountant keeping you out of an audit, or a financial advisor getting paid a commission to manage your money. But there are more efficient ways to leverage the skills and experiences of these professionals. You can pay people hourly for advice and ideas — with no promise of any services or product sales. You can put professionals on a retainer (at a discounted hourly rate) as part of your "quasi-family office." You're can also partner with your investment and insurance professionals to find ways to lower fees or even make money in areas that were once expenses for you. In all these cases, we can eliminate conflicts of interest, so everyone is rowing in the same direction for you.

As you adopt these new philosophies, I am confident that you will be well on your way to reaching your ambitious goals, but there is one step left. Please continue to the 7th Path — so you can get moving, and keep moving, in the direction of your dreams.

7th PATH
Achieving Your Desired Giraffluence

"My 3-step formula for success: get up early, work hard, strike oil."
—J. Paul Getty, once the world's richest man.

If you are serious about elevating your level of wealth, you will have to change course and take a different path. I wouldn't be a mathematician if I didn't give you a very simple formula I learned from a good friend of mine, Jack Canfield (***Chicken Soup for the Soul*** and ***The Success Principles***). It is so simple, which is what makes it so powerful:

E	+	R	=	O
Event	+	Response	=	Outcome

You want a different outcome. If you didn't, you wouldn't be reading this book. Perhaps you want financial freedom, greater success and respect, or the ability to help change the world as a philanthropist. Regardless of your motivation, you will have to change your responses to the current events, circumstances and people around you to get where you want to go.

It is natural to be resistant to change. It is common to fear the unknown. It's human to want to avoid being laughed at or criticized. All of these feelings are combined and amplified when you are trying something new. It's very similar to learning to walk or ride a bike. You will lose your balance and fall — a lot!

How a giraffe spends it first minutes of life, how it is built, and how it lives give you valuable insights into how to change your mindset, your actions, and your support system. These things will be integral to your transformation as you discover, and pursue, better paths toward your future elevated wealth.

For more updated information, and for other forms of education and support, I have created www.GiraffeUniversity.com. There are podcasts, video courses, articles and others interactive tools available for you. I have also asked many of my colleagues from the world of finance, entrepreneurship, and transformation to help. Please visit www.GiraffeUniversity.com to make sure you don't miss anything.

Chapter 34
Somebody Will Make It Big. Why Not You?

"Whether you think you can, or you think you can't, you're right!"
—Henry Ford

You may feel like a wildebeest or a zebra, lost in a herd, with no control over your future. When you spend your entire day with your head in the weeds eating, you don't have the opportunity to look to the horizon and visualize a better future for yourself. You may have a mountain of debt or feel the overwhelming financial responsibility for a family that has an endless capacity to always spend more than you earn. Maybe you are so busy taking care of people around you or working in your current job that you can't imagine having the time to do anything else. No matter how helpless you feel, there is a way off the beaten path to your elevated wealth.

Lottery or Lot of Desire?

On November 31, 2016, Fortune magazine reported, "1,700 People in America are Becoming Millionaires Every Day." This information was shared from a Bloomberg report that was based on projections from Boston Consulting Group. Spectrem Group's research of investors under 50 years of age with assets greater than $25 million reported that 73 percent cited inheritance as a factor in their success. Though that is a large percentage, this is very encouraging to those of us who don't believe we have an inheritance coming our way. A full 27 percent of investors who have more than $25 million in assets didn't see inheritance as a factor! In my head, I am hearing Jim Carrey's character (Lloyd Christmas) from *Dumb and Dumber* saying, "So you say I have a chance?"

Do you want more proof that you can make it, and make it big? *Forbes* reported 195 new billionaires in the world in 2017 (March 20, 2017). In *LoveMoney's* report from June of 2017, it reported a record 233 new entries to the billionaire club. You don't have to "wait for your time" either. Consider this shortlist of young billionaires:

Youngest Billionaires in America

Name	*Age*	*Net Worth*	*Source*
Kylie Jenner	22 years old	$1.0 billion	Kylie Cosmetics
Evan Spiegel	29 years old	$1.9 billion	Snap Inc.
Bobby Murphy	31 years old	$1.9 billion	Snap Inc.
Lukas Walton	33 years old	$18.4 billion	Walmart
Santo Domingo	34 years old	$1 billion	beverage
Mark Zuckerberg	35 (reached at 23)	$55 billion	Facebook
Dustin Moskovitz	35 years old	$9.3 billion	Facebook/Asana
Chris Wanstrath	35 years old	$1.4 billion	GitHub
Nathan Biecharczyk	36 years old	$4.1 billion	Airbnb
Kevin Systrom	36 years old	$1.3 billion	Instagram
RJ Scaringe	36 years old	$1.0 billion	Automotive
Scott Duncan	36 years old	$3.6 billion	Oil
Lynsi Snyder	37 years old	$3.6 billion	In-N-Out Burger
Drew Houston	37 years old	$1.3 billion	Dropbox
Brian Armstrong	37 years old	$1.0 billion	Coinbase

Chart created from data in Business Insider, 4/7/2020

This information should be very encouraging. You can become very successful by doing it yourself. You can even become a billionaire if you don't have a lot of money. If these *"youngins"* can acquire the wealth with fewer than fifteen years of adulthood, you should realize that this journey doesn't have to be an epic one that will take an entire lifetime.

You can't win if you don't play!

"Fortune sides with him who dares."

—Virgil

Keeping with the theme of the last segment of this chapter, I included the motto of the Vermont state lottery in 1985. This was also mimicked by many other lotteries, casinos and maybe even a few bookies.

According to the Tax Policy Center, there were 1,128,000 taxpayers earning over $400,000 per year. Approximately 115,000 people earn at least $10,000,000 per year. If you add up all the professional athletes in the United States, there are fewer than 10,000 of them. I estimate that ten percent of the athletes earn more than $10M per year. Aha! We just found 1,000 of the 115,000 we were hoping to identify. Where are the other 114,000 people who earn $10M per year? I am in the high net worth space as a sought-after advisor. I have probably met 100-200 of them. With that unique experience, I still can't tell you where to easily locate any large groups of those big earners in any state, let alone in yours.

This is a key observation for any giraffe setting out on an adventure. There is no clear, simple path to reaching the highest levels of success. However, you did learn important philosophies of the most successful and over 25 practical ideas that you can incorporate into your own journey

Charting a Better Path

Those who have catapulted their way from the top one percent into the top 0.1 percent have not done it by following any playbook. If there were a playbook, everyone in the top one percent would be at that level – and that is mathematically impossible. The most successful people in our country achieved that level of success because they saw an opportunity that others didn't. Their elevated perspective allowed them to see a better path, by doing something nobody had ever done before or by doing something others do, just doing it much better, faster or cheaper.

Most importantly, for most readers, you saw examples of self-made billionaires who are under the age of forty. You don't, in fact, need to have money to make money. You don't even need to have money to make a billion dollars in less than ten years. You can make a lot of money and you can make it in a relatively short time – with some luck, some dedication, and with a whole new mindset about money.

The most important thing is for you to take the next step. Yes, it might be scary. What the hell did you think it was going to be? You want more out of life. You are going to have to give up on a life that is not completely fulfilling. When you think about it, what are you really giving up?

Chapter 35
Lady Luck Favors the Bold: Give Yourself a Chance

"Like billions of giraffes before you, you too will survive the drop."
—Chris Jarvis

All change is startling, but a giraffe learns this at the earliest possible age. Imagine yourself as a baby giraffe — before its born. A warm and comfortable 15-month gestation period comes to a very abrupt ending. A short, but disruptive 1-hour labor may seem a bit hurried, but that isn't the worst of it. Giraffes are so committed to maintaining their elevated perspective that they even give birth standing up. This may be safer for the mother giraffe, but not so much for the baby who experiences a precipitous six-foot drop from mom to the hard earth below. Before the baby giraffe can adjust its eyes to its first glimpse of the blinding sunlight, it gets to experience one of the three fears humans possess at birth.

The newborn giraffe experiences the fear of falling, as it is dropped six to eight feet to the ground. Motion sickness, blinding light, helpless falling, and an abrupt jolt as he or she gets its first taste of gravity — these are all experienced within the first two hours of a giraffe's life. As startling as that initiation to life is, the giraffe instinctually knows to get up and get moving right away. If it doesn't, it will be the target of a predator.

A baby giraffe is six feet tall and weighs only 250 lbs. This doesn't make the giraffe particularly susceptible to smaller predators like jackals and fox, but it is very susceptible to hyenas, lions and even wild dogs. When it stands up for the first time, the baby giraffe will undoubtedly wobble on those skinny, undeveloped legs. The baby giraffe will fall down a few times before it gathers itself and learns to balance. The first few steps will be awkward and uncomfortable. This is expected, as those legs have been folded up in utero.

The baby giraffe has never stood, let alone walked, before this moment. Why would you expect the giraffe to do anything other than struggle, stumble and even fall?

As crazy as this whole ordeal sounds, this is how billions of giraffes have started their lives over the last million years. They all survived the drop – and you will too. You have to shake off the confusion, get up, wobble, and get moving. Today!

Find a Guide When You're Lost

Your journey is going to take through unfamiliar territory. You will get lost. You will make mistakes. As you take greater risks, you will also have large setbacks and suffer greater losses. This is all part of the process. You are going to have to rely on your GPS – Giraffe Positioning System. This is not an electronic device, but a support system that will help you when you need it most.

I remember when my first marriage was failing. My dad was such a big help. I don't know how I would have gotten through it without him. I can remember a particularly difficult conversation. He asked me what I was really afraid of in getting divorced. I felt awful telling him that I didn't want to get divorced and end up alone – like he was. It always bothered me that such a great guy never remarried, but saying it felt like I was calling him a failure. He wasn't hurt. He gave me the most amazing advice, "Chris. My life has not turned out how I wanted it to, but that doesn't make me a failure. I made choices that gave me the best chance to be happy. The fact that they didn't work out doesn't mean my choices were wrong. You have to make decisions that give you a chance to be happy and never look back."

You want to find people who will support you and will encourage you to pursue what is important to you. The most powerful ways to do this are:

1) **Communities of like-minded people.** This could be a private Facebook group, a men's or women's group, or some other group that is committed to helping each other reach the same types of goals. The energy from the large group will offer a significant volume of encouraging comments and stories. If you

visit www.GiraffeUniversity.com, you will see a link to a free Facebook group.

2) **Mastermind group.** This is a small group usually consisting of 7 to 15 people. It is much more intimate than the community, so you can be more vulnerable, get to know the people more closely, and you can have more impact on each other. This group should meet at least once per quarter, possibly once per month. The highlight of my entrepreneurial career was being in my CEO group for over 9 years. For more information, please visit www.GiraffeUniversity.com/company/resources.
3) **Accountability partner.** This is a one-on-one relationship. The two of you share your goals and interact daily. The interaction is usually a text or an email at the start of the day. The communication is of the five most important tasks you have for your day. The next day, you start with which of the previous day's five you did, and what the next day's five are. I had great success in my own personal transformation with my amazing accountability partner, Mayor Preet Didbal of Yuba City, California. I highly recommend this step for everyone.

Put Your Heart into This

One interesting thing about the giraffe is that it has the largest heart of the land mammal world. It takes 24 pounds of muscle to pump all that blood up the long neck. This lifeblood is what fuels the brain, giving the giraffe the opportunity to leverage its elevated perspective to see better paths.

As I finish this book, I am also mourning the loss of my dad. Ray Jarvis passed away just two weeks ago. Despite the coronavirus chaos, I was lucky enough to spend the last few weeks of his life with him. Given that this loss is so recent, what I am about to share is very meaningful to me. Death has a way of helping me take an honest inventory of my life. I find it much easier to say "no" and to throw away things in my garage, office, and closet than I did a month ago. I can see things more clearly as I revisit the great advice he gave me and recalculate my own path going forward. This is the silver lining for me, and I am eternally grateful.

I highly encourage you to come back to this book, and especially to this section, to review important ways for you to get started on your journey, get back on track, or to speed up your progress – so you can give yourself the best possible chance for you to be happy with your finances and with your life.

Be the Giraffe!

Chris Jarvis, MBA, CFP®

Chris Jarvis helps entrepreneurs and families discover unique paths to unconventional success. He has written sixteen books, including the bestseller, *6 Secrets to Leveraging Success: A Guide for Entrepreneurs, Family Offices, and Their Trusted Advisors.*

Chris proudly sits on the advisory board of the prestigious IC^2 Institute at the University of Texas-Austin and the Dean's Advisory Council for the University of South Carolina School of Medicine. He also sits on the boards of the National Coalition for Safe Schools, Streamline Miami, and Angel City Sports.

Chris is a financial advisor for high net worth clients, a marketing and sales guru, and the VP of Strategic Partnerships for the Canfield Training Group. Chris has been quoted in *The Wall Street Journal* and been a guest on *Bloomberg Personal Finance.*

He founded Giraffe University™ to help business owners and future entrepreneurs See Differently and Business Differently.

www.ChrisJarvis.me

www.GiraffeUniversity.com

Acknowledgements

I want to thank my parents Dot Fogarty and Ray Jarvis for, always believing in me, encouraging me, and, most of all, for teaching me the importance of taking care of those who are less fortunate. I want to thank my sister, Jennifer Hill for keeping me grounded and focused on what's important, even when I tried very hard to lose sight. My wife, Heather, for putting up with my countless shifts in focus and listening to my changing pitch over and over again. For my kids, Chloe, Kierstin, and Tyler who show me why I do what I do.

I want to thank Jack Canfield and Patty Aubery for making me put the giraffe on paper. Dan Stanley for encouraging me to see the importance of getting my message out. Scott Spiewak and Holt Vaughn for helping me release my inner giraffe. Ramon Peralta, Amanda Barnes, and the team at Peralta Design for the awesome cover and web graphics. Rick Petry for leading me and watching over me like a mother. Cathleen Elle and Deb Sandella for boldly going where so few people would dare go, to keep me sane. Cindy Hochart for taking on the herculean task of editing my crazy work. Lastly and mostly, for Mike Loomis – the man who did a lot of the heavy lifting, so many of the small things, and filled in everywhere in between. This book and Giraffe University would only be ideas if not for you, my friend. Thank you.

A special thank you to fellow giraffes who helped launch this book on release day. Your support means the world to me.

Ryan Abitz
Ian Benedict
William Bronson
George Brown
Maddie Brown
Susan Brown
Amy Burton
Filissa Caserta
Mike Colburn
Philip Daunt
Cathleen Elle
Catherine Engmann
Shannon Faulkner
Stuart Brian Fields
Tammy Gibson
Gregory Goeders
Ira Gottshall
Laura Hamilton
Matthew Jarret
Paula Harris
Hanna Hermanson
Cindy Hochart
Louise Hoeyer
Randy Hudson
Tom Jelke
Johannys Jimenez-Hartog
Mohanjit Jolly
Nicholas Lamparelli
Audra Lavoie
Edward Ledford
Grace Liang
Mallorie Manosh
Michael Maske
Sherry McCool
Dorota McKay
Gwen Medved
Allie Miller
Pam Miller
Marilyn Montgomery
Jim Munroe
Jeanette Paxia
Rick Petry
Ramon Peralta
Sunil Parekh
Ati Rexroad
Samantha Ruth
Mari-Liis Sallo
Mark Hugh Sam
Deb Sandella
Denise Schickel
Dick Schuettner
Lorna Scott
Melissa Shea
Scott Silvers
Bob Sollazzo
Dan Stanley
J. Holly Stevens
Maggie Sullivan
Rupali Trehan
Mike Tesoriero
Nelly Torras
Aparna Vemuri
Paul Wilson
Wendy Witt
Carole Young
Blake Zaal

Ready to Work Less, Earn More, and Enjoy Your Wealth?

Chris Jarvis helps business owners and wealthy families reach and enjoy higher levels of success, by taking a different path.

You may be like many of Chris's previous clients, if you want to know:

- What must I change to minimize stress and maximize income?
- Where do I leave my kids inheritance, so they don't get lazy or lose it in divorce?
- How can I save millions in unnecessary taxes over my lifetime?
- How do I get employees to act like owners without giving them equity in my company?
- What makes my company worth millions more to a buyer?
- Who can I hire to help, who doesn't have something to sell?
- What are your richest clients doing that I should be doing too?

For decades, Chris has helped successful professionals, entrepreneurs, and even billionaire families build, protect, and transfer significant wealth. If you want to get more out of your hard work, you have to find a better path.

When you See Differently, you can Money Differently.

Contact Chris at www.ChrisJarvis.me

Special Offer for Financial, Legal and Tax Advisors

Do you, or would you like to, serve high net worth clients?

Chris's books and articles have generated over 10,000 physician, business owner and family office leads. He sits on the advisory boards of the University of South Carolina School of Medicine, the IC^2 Institute at the University of Texas-Austin and has worked with three billionaire families.

After selling his financial firm for millions of dollars in 2016, Chris turned his attention to teaching others. He has consulted, trained, and mentored hundreds of professionals on advanced transactions, sales and marketing, lead-generating communications, and practice-building.

If you want to learn how to work and worry less, while earning and building more for yourself, your firm, and your family, you must find a better path.

When you See Differently, you can Business Differently.

Interested in having Chris help you with your business and clients?

Contact Chris at www.ChrisJarvis.me

There is no EntrepreneUrship without *You*, the Entrepreneur.

If your company doesn't reflect your unique character, you are on the long—wrong—road to success.

Why is this important?

Starting a business is difficult. Growing a business is even harder. If you focus on profits and forget about yourself, you may end up like I did. Until I saw a better path, I referred to my business as the prison I built—then I locked the gate with me on the inside.

If you don't want to be a prisoner to your company, to your clients, to your employees, or to your own success, you have to focus on the delicate balance of:

Your Company Your Cash Your Character

Elevate Your Perspective and See a Better Path for You and Your Company

See Differently. Business Differently.

Chris Jarvis

Founder and President www.GiraffeUniversity.com

Made in the USA
Monee, IL
22 January 2023

25925261R00144